MONEY MAGICALLY

MONEY MAGICALLY
30 DAYS OF PROGRAMMING, PROCESSING, AND MAGIC TO CREATE AND MANIFEST MONEY

ANNE SAYERS

SYNERGY TRAINING INSTITUTE

Copyright © 2017 by Anne Singer Sayers
All rights reserved. This book or any portion thereof may not be reproduced or used in any manner whatsoever without the express written permission of the publisher except for the use of brief quotations in a book review.

Printed in the United States of America

First Printing, 2017

ISBN-13:
978-0692883181 (Money Magically)

ISBN-10: 0692883185

Synergy Training Institute
P.O. Box 1693
Thousand Oaks CA 91358

CONTENTS

Introduction vii
From the Author xi

Day 1 – Congratulations 1
Day 2 – Building a Wealth Resonance 5
Day 3 – Discovering Limiting Beliefs 11
Day 4 – Burning Desire 17
Day 5 – Your Ideal Day 25
Day 6 – Your Money Matrix 31
Day 7 – Your Earning Pattern 37
Day 8 – Changing Beliefs 45
Day 9 – Power of the Subconscious 57
Day 10 – Building Resonance 63
Day 11 – Resistances 67
Day 12 – Making It Real 75
Day 13 – Self-image 85
Day 14 – I'll See It When I Believe It 91
Day 15 – Stepping Up – The Art of Manifesting 99
Day 16 – Deserving 111
Day 17 – Power of the Future 119
Day 18 – Motivation 125
Day 19 – Avenue of Manifestation 137
Day 20 – Dancing with Angels 145
Day 21 – Gratitude 155
Day 22 – Rounding Third 163
Day 23 – Who You Are Becoming 171
Day 24 – Modeling 179
Day 25 – Your New Script 187
Day 26 – Fear Standoff 195
Day 27 – Holding the Frequency 207
Day 28 – Developing an Abundance Routine 215
Day 29 – Self-Forgiveness 221
Day 30 – Open Your Heart 229

Conclusion	237
Appendix 1 – Visualizations	241
Appendix II – Affirmations	245
Appendix III – How Rich People Think	247

INTRODUCTION

Even though everyone wants it, money is the one thing no one talks about. If you have too much of it, others might be jealous. If you have too little of it, you may be embarrassed. And, if you don't have enough of it, you live in fear. If that isn't confusing enough, you are also told *"Don't be fearful!" "Don't complain!" "Don't brag!"* and, most of all, *"Don't you dare tell anyone you want a ton of it!"* That's just plain shocking!

Is it any wonder, that money is a struggle?

What do you know about manifesting? What do you know about consciously choosing to create something you want and then using the tools you have mentally, emotionally and physically to create exactly what you want? You are going to have an opportunity to dig down deep and make changes at a subliminal level like you have never done before. For the next 30 days, you will be guided on a journey to not just explore money, but to manifest more money than you ever thought possible! No more complaining about it. Setting a goal and sticking to it. Demanding what you want with a new fury. No longer being ashamed, embarrassed, or worrying about what others think. If you want money - demand it!

Claim it! And then you can manifest it and start living life with all the bounty that is available to everyone!

You may say you've already worked with your *abundance* issues; that you've taken lots of courses with little or no success, but it is time to put all that aside. It's time to start creating exactly what you want and it starts by admitting that you want it!

You will be visualizing, meditating, affirming, and focusing on the one thing you were told to just create and not think about. In the next 30 days, you are going to be thinking about it, talking about it, and resonating on it with the goal of creating it. A LOT OF IT! You will be led to learn, explore, and employ powerful techniques to program a whole new reality.

In this book, you will find visualizations, meditations, and daily exercises to expand your self-image and build a resonance of wealth. Can you imagine where you will be in 30 or 60 or 180 days, when you've been focusing all your energy and attention on accomplishing your money goals? Through this book, you can be totally immersed in reaching your money goals by sensing, imagining, and ultimately believing that you are a millionaire, a multi-millionaire, even a billionaire, whatever level your self-image can handle. You can stretch your "money image" until you not only believe you are wealthy, but KNOW you are! And then the fun begins as gifts and surprises start showing up in your reality confirming that a new resonance is at work. People have reported things such as checks arriving in the mail, unexpected refunds showing up, interest rates going down on their mortgage and credit cards, finding dollars and coins in the middle of the sidewalk, and an overall increase in income and savings in a very short period of time. But, that is just the beginning!

Can you imagine what will happen when you focus all your attention on manifesting money? How will you feel when you visualize and imagine a $1,000,000 bank statement or multiple checks for $100,000

INTRODUCTION

each? It's time to step into your magical cloak and use the power of your mind to build a resonance that can create more money than you ever thought possible.

Are you up to the task? Are you willing to put your knowledge to work focusing on prosperity, focusing on abundance to move beyond limiting beliefs to create and manifest money? Are you willing to make a commitment with no going back? Because that is the kind of commitment it takes. Not just for 30 days, but for the rest of your life! If you're ready, then let's get started!

FROM THE AUTHOR

They say money is the easiest thing to create, yet, so many of us struggle for it or live most of our lives barely making enough. If you are like me and have been studying metaphysics for a long time, you already know a great deal about reality creation and taking charge of your life. You also already know that your beliefs are the root of all your issues around money. Often these are beliefs around deserving, beliefs that money is bad or "dirty" and that wanting money means you are selfish or greedy or just not *spiritual*. These limiting beliefs are not only false, but are at the core of what hinders and blocks your ability to truly be abundant. Even with all the knowledge and wisdom you may have gleaned over the years, it is not so easy to find such beliefs and discover what keeps holding you back. That is why I wrote this book, with the goal of being so totally immersed in your desire and goals for abundance that you begin to resonate at a whole new level.

About ten years ago, I began visualizing piles of money stacked all around the room. I repeated the same exercise every day for three weeks and started receiving checks in my mail box. In total, I received over $15,000 in a period of only 30 days! I look back on that experience that confirmed that I know how to manifest money, but then, of course, I

FROM THE AUTHOR

found myself asking, *"Why did I stop?"*

A lot of things got in the way over the years including getting lost in the busyness and the conflicts of life, but most of all, developing a lot of fears on whether it was "okay" to have an abundant, prosperous life. But now, it is all different. Regardless of what so many people may say, money is one of the more important goals in life. No matter how much we may argue, money is a life changer. If we don't have it, life can be filled with pain and struggle, but when we do have it, we can begin to have a heck of a lot of fun AND help a heck of a lot of people! This just may be the opportunity you've been looking for all this time to really turn your life into a positive direction of great wealth.

You may have heard the expression, *"It is only a belief away!"* I believe this maxim unequivocally and have seen the results in my own life as well as in that of so many others who have read this book. Knowledge is wonderful, and we all have a lot of that, but what I and so many others want is results. What we all want is to take that knowledge and put it to work in our lives in a positive way. What fun and satisfaction it is to consciously create success and abundance by choice!

So, I created this 30 day program to assist you in this exploration, to assist you in finding the bottom line of beliefs that you hold around money, wealth, or even success and to provide techniques and processes to assist in moving beyond all such limitations to create unlimited success.

For the next 30 days, or however long you choose, you are going to be exploring yourself and your own beliefs at a deep level. You may be very surprised at what you discover! But discovering the limiting beliefs is just the first step. Next, you need to change the beliefs and there are lots of techniques available to assist you to do just that!

You will discover that rich people are no different than the rest of us. They just hold different beliefs about money! You now have a chance to change your beliefs and give yourself permission to be more than

FROM THE AUTHOR

comfortable, but to be wealthy! This course is a real eye opener and a life changer! More than that, you truly can change your money pattern and become the millionaire you were always meant to be!

My most urgent advice! Don't quit. Keep going until you complete every chapter and every exercise – even if it takes you far more than 30 days to do so. People who failed at this program are the ones who weren't committed in the first place or who stopped mid-stream and never finished. Don't let that be you! This is a golden opportunity to change your entire life in a positive way and all you have to do is stick to the plan!

Anne

DAY 1
CONGRATULATIONS

You know that expression:" All *great deeds start with a few small steps!"* You've made the first step, expressing interest in this book and embracing an opportunity to change your money issues forever. But it takes far more than just buying and reading a book. It takes real conviction and determination to keep going, even when you get scared; even when you fall down.

To succeed in this program, you need to make a firm commitment to yourself today to stick to the program. If you have spent a lifetime in a resonance of restriction, reaffirming beliefs of limitation and lack, it is time to change it. In order to change it, you need to reprogram your subconscious which has been assisting you to create a limited financial reality. Can you imagine what will happen when you start releasing restrictive beliefs, replacing them with empowered, unlimited ones? Can you imagine the possibilities when you spend 30 days resonating on new beliefs, such as:

- *Money is the easiest thing in the world to create*
- *I am wealthy beyond what I ever thought possible*
- *I always have plenty of money*

DAY 1

- *I have more money than I can spend in a lifetime*
- *I can buy anything I want*
- *Being wealthy is bringing me great freedom and fun*

Studies have shown that goals that get reached are those that are firm, well-defined, and to which you are completely committed. Therefore, if you want to succeed in creating a life that is free from financial limitation, you need to set a goal to devote your attention and energy 100%. Make a commitment now to complete the daily exercises and finish the program. In purchasing this book, you are indicating a desire to change, but now it is time to commit to changing the way you have always done things and the way you have always thought and related to money. Before we go any further, stop now and make a commitment to yourself. Write down the words listed below (or something similar) in your own handwriting and sign your name at the end. This is your first commitment to your new life.

> *Dear Self,*
>
> *I am ready to change my life and move into a life of financial freedom and bounty. I am ready to receive great riches and to release limitations that have kept me living a less than abundant life. I am excited about my future where I am wealthy beyond anything I ever thought possible. I commit to follow through on this program for the next 30 days to the end.*
>
> *Even though I may waiver and even though I may hit resistances, I am committed to keep going forward until I have accomplished my goal.*
>
> *Dated this ___ day of _____, 20___.*

Make sure you sign your name at the end of the above commitment and put it in a place where you will see it daily. To enhance your progress, convert the above statements into an affirmation that you repeat as many times as you can remember throughout your day. This is your first homework and an important first step. Make the commitment now!

EXERCISE 1
COMMITMENT STATEMENT & STATEMENT OF DESIRE

1. Your first exercise is to get a journal and write out your commitment statement. You can copy the version on page 2 or write your own version. Make sure you sign it as this is now a binding contract.

2. Next, write out your Statement of Desire which is a bit different. Spend some time thinking about your overall financial goals. What is it you want to accomplish and in what time period? Give yourself some time to think about this and write it as a single statement using your notebook or journal. This is something you are going to refer to daily. Here are some examples:

"I am completely out of debt and creating over $_____ a year in income."
"I am a multi-millionaire with $_____ net worth."
"I am earning $_____ by _____ (date.)"
"By_____ [date], I have accumulated over $_____."
"I have over $_____ in my savings account by _____ (date.)"

When you have found the "statement of your desire" that feels right - write it down on a 3 x 5 card or a sturdy piece of paper and then make sure you read it to yourself **every day - TWICE A DAY.** Enter what you did today and what observations you have made in your personal notebook or journal.

DAY 2

BUILDING A WEALTH RESONANCE

To get started on building resonance toward your new money goal, you need to start finding things that *"tickle your fancy,"* as the expression goes. Start thinking about things you want and how good it feels to know you can create any of those things in your life. We are starting with money, but this process works for anything you want to manifest. Recently, a friend told me about an event where she met a handsome movie star and it prompted a conversation about programming this man as part of her future. At first, we each hit the *"no way"* energy, but if you keep playing with an idea, eventually you start to expand on the *possibility*. Remember the phrase, "Anything's possible!"

Keeping that in mind, the goal is to keep stretching your imagination and belief system to explore and accept that anything is possible. If you can manifest a job that pays you $3000 a month, for example, how would you feel if you were receiving $6,000 a month? $10,000 a month? $30,000 a month? Usually, the first response is "*No* ...." and then, after a few moments, it turns to "*Really?*" It's the "*really*" part that begins to stir not only your imagination, but excitement and hope.

The goal for the next 30 days is to continue to focus on anything that

DAY 2

stirs these energies of excitement, hope, desire, passion, enthusiasm, and joy! As you think about this, start giving yourself permission to think about something you have always wanted. Perhaps it is a vacation to Paris or a cruise to Tahiti. Perhaps it is a new home or a new car. A private plane? A yacht? Quitting your job and moving to Costa Rica? Start with something you have always wanted to have and play with the idea that it is already yours. Notice how you feel as a result of just pretending you have it.

Once you begin to generate a feeling of enthusiasm and excitement about having that *thing*, continue to build on that feeling by expanding the thoughts and adding more ideas to it. For example, if you want to acquire a million dollars, start first by imagining what having a million dollars would feel like. How do you imagine receiving the million dollars? Is it a check that arrives in the mail? Do you find yourself with a winning lottery ticket? Is there some kind of invention or idea that you have that sells for $1,000,000?

> *Actor Jim Carrey often talks about how he wrote himself a check for $10,000,000 for "acting services rendered." He visualized this check for years and in 1997, he received a check for $10,000,000 for his role in the film Dumb and Dumber.*[1]

When you discover that "thing" or idea that "excites you most," keep thinking about it. Keep telling yourself that this is something you can have until you believe it. Use your imagination as the powerful tool it is by imagining yourself on that yacht or laying on the beach in Tahiti, or signing the papers to purchase your dream house.

Go online and start shopping yachts or vacation homes or your dream

---

[1] Jim Carrey told this story on the Oprah Show in 1997. You'll also find numerous articles about it online. www.oprah.com/oprahs-lifeclass/what-oprah-learned-from-jim-carrey-video

car. Whatever it is that generates this energy of excitement is what you will use to build your resonance of wealth.

Building a resonance of wealth is about these four important things:

1. Maintaining a SINGLE-MINDED FOCUS on what you want to achieve
2. Focusing your attention CONSISTENTLY on your goals
3. Continuously EXPANDING your imagination and beliefs of what is possible
4. PERSISTING in your efforts until your goal is reached

Thus, FOCUS, CONSISTENCY, EXPANSION, and PERSISTANCE are going to be your tools for, at the very least, the next 30 days, but hopefully, for the rest of your life! In the next section, we will be developing a plan of action; steps and habits that you will consistently follow to maintain this single focus. When you do this, the habits eventually take over and eventually make the continuous resonance of wealth operate automatically all the time.

EXERCISE 2

WHAT WILL YOU DO WITH YOUR NEW-FOUND MILLIONS?

In this exercise, you are going to start planning what you are going to do when you receive the money you have set as your goal. Assuming it is millions of dollars, what will you do first? Pay off bills? Pay off credit cards? Buy a new car? If you are going to pay off bills, how will you do that? Write a check? Set up payment in your online banking account? If so, imagine that you are sitting at your desk with your check book or at your computer. Look up the exact amount of the bill or credit card or auto loan and write a check for that amount. Imagine you are writing the address on the envelope and placing the check in the envelope. See yourself put a stamp on it and walk to the mail box to drop it in the mail. Feel how good it feels to have that bill paid off. Then do it with the next bill until they are all paid off. Emotionally feel the release and the freedom. You just paid off $----- worth of debt! Celebrate it, but most importantly, feel it and then write out how you feel in your notebook or journal.

1. Now, that you have manifested the money that you desire, write on a separate piece of paper or in your journal what you do first with the money. Write it in present tense. Here's an example:

   I just paid off a $8,753 credit card bill. I feel so great! I am going this afternoon to look at new cars. I want to buy a convertible, and will be checking out Audi, Mercedes and Lexus. I am so excited. My life is amazing!

2. Make a list of all of the things you want to buy and do with your new-

found millions. Make the list thorough. For example, if you want to remodel your house, start researching online for the kind of floors you want, the kind of windows or doors you want. Get detailed and include everything you can think of that you want. If it is a vacation or a vacation home, include where it is, what it looks like, the climate, the landscape, the furnishings, etc. Write out what you discover.

3. Write out how you feel after having paid off every single debt, credit card, auto loan, even your current mortgage!

4. Make note of the ways you hold yourself back from spending money. For example, do you not buy something because of price? Do you avoid certain stores because you think "they're too expensive?" When you buy gas for your car do you shop for the cheapest station? As a multi-millionaire, you no longer have to be concerned about what you buy or how much you spend. Write out what you've discovered in your notebook or journal.

5. Continue to imagine each thing you will do with your millions. If you want to buy a new car, start shopping online. Go to car dealerships and start getting all the details on the car you want to purchase. Remember - money is no object! Pick out any car you want. Then imagine you have that car. Imagine when you are driving you are in your new car. Smell the leather. Feel your hands on the steering wheel. Feel the joy of driving your dream car. Go to the stores that have the products you want. Go to open houses in the neighborhoods where you would like to live. Test drive the cars you want to own. Once you begin to change the way you think and feel with regard to money and the things you can do with it, you will begin to feel excited, looking forward to the future when you will receive the money you have set as your goal. Write out all you have discovered including how great it feels to be rich.

DAY 3
DISCOVERING LIMITING BELIEFS

The art of manifesting is based on a consistent flow of energy that is produced by your thoughts and feelings. You are already doing this, but most often you are not aware of the beliefs that are behind the energy you are currently generating. You can look at your reality and see evidence of these beliefs. This realization may not be new to you, but what is new is that you have an opportunity now to change your resonance to that of a person who consistently generates huge sums of money. People who are financially successful don't apologize for the fact that they make a lot of money. They are proud of it and embrace it and consistently reach toward opportunities for more. If you are honest with yourself, you will recognize and acknowledge that you hold back from truly embracing all the abundance that is available to you.

- Do you feel ashamed to say you want money?
- Are you embarrassed to admit that you want a LOT of money?
- Are you ashamed that you have difficulty making money?

Many religions and cultures judge money as something bad and often those very cultures are the ones that have millions of people who are

DAY 3

starving and living in poverty. Historically, it was wise for the wealthy nobility to tell the masses of poor people that they would get their rewards later in heaven. But do you *really* believe that? If you do, do you want to continue to believe that?

If you go online and start looking for quotes about *wealth*, most of what you will find will be statements such as *"Money can't buy you happiness," "Money is the root of all evil,"* and even *"You must let go of all material goods"* to be truly spiritual. It's time to examine these messages and make a choice of whether you want to continue to believe such things or are ready to release them and open to embrace a bountiful life.

People who are truly wealthy don't carry any of these baseless beliefs. Do you honestly believe that having a lot of money will make you unhappy? In truth, unlimited wealth gives you greater freedom to enjoy life, to fulfill your destiny, and to take your talents, wisdom, and skills out into the world to assist others to enjoy the same freedom and happiness. To do otherwise, means you will stay in the same place where you have always been, limited, hiding, and often unhappy.

Ask yourself the question, *"Why?"* Why would anyone want to do that? People who have great wealth are enjoying life. They are not worrying whether they can buy something nor are they holding themselves back from buying something or refraining from doing something for *fear* they won't have *enough*.

They are enjoying every minute of their lives and the freedom that wealth provides. Is money a panacea that will solve all problems? Of course not, but in order to allow yourself to reach for the freedom and happiness that great wealth can provide, you need to let go of the limiting beliefs that keep you down and hold you back.

Open to the possibilities. Give yourself full permission to have all the money you could ever want so you can do whatever you want to do without restriction. No doubt there are people who have goals for wealth that are selfish and greedy, but is that you? If so, you probably would not be reading this book. What a person does with the wealth they have or what they do to obtain it is about their personal character, not about money or wealth itself. There are many people who use their wealth to assist others in need; who develop their own charities and donate tremendous amounts of money to wonderful causes. Which one will you choose to be?

It is a true axiom that what you focus upon will expand and grow. Therefore, if you focus upon lack and limitation that is what you will experience. Likewise, if you focus on abundance, that is also what you will experience. You may already know this. This book isn't about teaching what you already know. It is about consistently reminding yourself of your goal and believing more and more that whatever you want, you can have. If you can manifest an increase in money, and even more so, manifest great wealth, what else can you do? The answer to that is ANYTHING!

So, what is your goal? Did you write out your Statement of Desire on Day One? Did you read it twice yesterday and then again today? If not, why not? Why would you stop yourself? Do you believe it won't work? Here is a quote from Napoleon Hill's famous and most widely read book *Think and Grow Rich*:

> *An educated man is not, necessarily, one who has an abundance of general or specialized knowledge. An educated man is one who has so developed the faculties of his mind that he may acquire anything he wants, or its equivalent, without violating the rights of others.*

Take some time today to contemplate how you really feel about having a lot of money. Do you feel anxious? Fearful? What beliefs do you think you hold that are making your feel that way? Write out these thoughts and feelings and don't forget that every day you are to remind yourself of your goals by reading your goal statement and re-reading the commitment you made to yourself in Chapter One. You are on your way to great wealth and that is a very exciting and worthwhile goal to stick to

DAY 3

and ultimately achieve!

EXERCISE 3

HOW DO YOU FEEL ABOUT BEING RICH?

From the time you were a tiny child, you have been taking in information and evaluating life, your world, and who you are. You have been trying to make sense of the people around you and have formed many, many conclusions and beliefs. In this exercise, you are going to start taking stock of the numerous beliefs you have formed about money, about wealth, and about your role in it. Using your journal or notebook, write out answers to the following questions:

1. If someone asked you how you feel about having a lot of money, what would you say?

2. Does it make a difference who is asking you? In other words, would you tell a stranger that it's not important, but tell your spouse or a close family member that you really do want money, or vice versa?

3. How do you feel about "wanting" money? Does it make you feel guilty? Ashamed? Embarrassed? Write out your thoughts and feelings.

4. Do you find yourself making judgments about people who live in mansions, drive expensive exotic cars, or who flaunt their money? If so, what things do you find yourself saying or thinking?

5. Do you find yourself wanting to hang out in places with wealthy people or do you do the opposite because you feel uncomfortable around wealthy people?

6. Write out what beliefs you think you must hold as a result of your answers to the above questions.

EXERCISE 3

7. Check out the list of "Money Beliefs" pages in Chapter 5 and start making a list of both the positive and negative beliefs you are discovering you hold around money and wealth. You might be surprised at what you discover.

DAY 4

BURNING DESIRE

In order to succeed in this program, and in order to succeed in accumulating great riches, you must have not only desire, but have a *burning* desire. It is apparent that you have a desire to have more money in your life or you wouldn't have purchased this book, but how strong is that desire? Studies have shown that rich people have a completely different way of thinking about success and looking at money. This crucial difference is what assures a future of success no matter what the goal and it starts with desire, not just any desire, but a *burning desire;* in fact, an *obsession*.

Now, when you read the word obsession, what kind of thoughts and feelings come up? Often, the suggestion that we should be obsessed with the goal of achieving great wealth is the very thing that can turn us away. We have been programmed from often well-meaning parents, teachers, and care givers that we should be satisfied with what we have and that obsession is a terrible thing and that *obsessing* about money is a terrible quality, even a sinful one. We are all programmed that an obsession is a sign of imbalance or sickness, but to the contrary, every great success or achievement that has ever happened in the world was rooted in an obsession to succeed. Merriam-Webster's Dictionary defines the term

DAY 4

obsession as follows:

> *a state in which someone thinks about someone or something constantly or frequently, especially in a way that is not normal.*

Notice the last part of the above definition "*especially in a way that is not normal.*" Is that the part that scares you, that it is not normal to be obsessed with money? But then, what is normal? According to statistics, only 2% of the world has attained great wealth. That means that the norm, the 98% normal population, live all of their lives in a range between just having enough to sheer poverty. But, as a seeker of truth or a self-growth junkie (as so many of us are), you have long lived beyond the norm. You have learned things and explored things that the average person, the *normal* person, would never believe in a thousand years. But that hasn't stopped you. Your passion for understanding how life works and for healing, growing, and changing has pushed you beyond the normal quest for knowledge. In fact, wouldn't you agree that your drive to grow and change is something you *think about constantly or frequently, especially in a way that is not normal?*

That is great news! You have an exceptional drive to become more and now you have an opportunity to become more in a very tangible way; in the creation of great wealth that will give you the opportunity to fulfill all of your dreams and desires. To succeed, you need to create a whole new way of seeing, relating, and thinking about money.

Steve Siebold, author of the book *How Rich People Think* and a self-made multi-millionaire, interviewed more than 1,200 of the world's wealthiest people over a period of 30 years. In his book, he states that the normal person

> *has been brainwashed to believe rich people are lucky or dishonest ... That's why there's a certain shame that comes along with 'getting rich in lower income communities.*

If you want to move out of the normal patterns of the average person, who seem to most often be worrying about money, then you need to honestly evaluate your thoughts and beliefs around not just having money, but BEING RICH and, in particular, being OBSESSED WITH BEING RICH.

What is the fear that runs beneath your hesitation to be exceedingly rich and having a goal of being obsessed with being rich? Most often, there is a fear that if you become obsessed with money, you will become the worst kind of human being - greedy, selfish, uncaring, even cruel. But, is that true? In your exploration of yourself and in all your years of growth and change, you have encountered many erroneous beliefs. You have seen the value of changing limiting beliefs and you have done so. Now, you have another opportunity to change beliefs that can totally alter everything in your life; for with money you will have opportunities to bring your desires into being. With great wealth, you can take action in the world using the immense knowledge and wisdom you have gained. You can be a part of birthing a new world that is destined to be!

Spend the rest of this day assessing and evaluating the beliefs you have around money, particularly around the idea of raising your *desire* to have money to a *burning desire*, even to an *obsession*. Work with anything that may limit your *obsession* to obtaining great wealth.

EXERCISE 4

CREATE A BURNING DESIRE

In this exercise, you are going to get more intimate with your desire for money. Answer the following questions.

1. On a scale from 1 to 10 - how high is your desire to have money?

_____

2. Does your level of desire change as you get more specific about your goal? For example, if your desire to have money is 8, does it go higher or lower when you desire to have a larger amount of money? (Be really honest with yourself.)

3. Using the same scale, rate the level of desire you have for each of the following amounts:

$1,000,000?	_____
$50,000,000?	_____
$100,000,000?	_____
$200,000,000?	_____
$1 billion	_____

4. Write how intensely you want money and how much you want to have. Include any feelings that came up when you imagined having each of the above amounts.

5. Do you feel guilty about having a lot of money? __ Yes __ No

6. Do you have fears about what other people will think if you have a lot of money? __ Yes __ No

7. Do you believe you will hurt someone (your father, your

mother, siblings, etc.), if you are more successful than them?
__ Yes __ No

8. Is the thought of being obsessed with money distasteful to you?
__ Yes __ No

9. What beliefs do you hold that cause such a response?

10. Now, write and write non-stop what you think and feel about the idea of being obsessed with money. Just let the words flow and flow and when you are done, go back and read what you wrote.

DAY 5
YOUR IDEAL DAY

How do you feel about money? When you think about money do you feel good? Are you grateful for the money you have right now? What kind of relationship do you have with money? As young children, we have no concept about money; what it means or how it works. Our first understanding about money comes from our parents or caregivers. What messages did they give you? **Were you told not to touch money because "money is dirty?" Were** you told if you wanted something you had to "save your money," but, you never really learned to save because when you finally had enough, you spent it all on the things you previously wanted? Did you learn that you could only have money if you worked hard? Sacrificed? Were you taught that money is more important than people because Dad always worked instead of spending time with you? Or, were you told that making money important is selfish or even sinful? Do you have beliefs that money depends on other people because you are powerless to make or earn your own money? Do you believe that to have money, you have to struggle and suffer? Do you believe that the only way to have money is to earn it doing work you don't enjoy?

As we have already been discussing, the beliefs you hold around and about money are important to discover and remove. They are already programmed into your subconscious and are at the basis of your current money pattern. Your subconscious is like a computer. It is constantly taking in and processing data. The operating system in this computer is based on beliefs you formed over many years about earning, about money, and about what it means to be wealthy. Check out the following list of negative beliefs and check the ones that apply to you.

__ God doesn't want me to have money
__ God wants us to struggle
__ God wants us to suffer
__ Having money is greedy
__ Having money makes you evil
__ Bad people don't deserve money
__ I can't have money
__ I'm not worthy of having money
__ I'm powerless over money
__ It's better to take less than be selfish
__ I just want enough to get by
__ It's not fair others have a lot of money
__ It's a hassle having money
__ It's bad to have money
__ It's bad to want money
__ It's impossible to make lots of money
__ It's more spiritual to be poor
__ Making money is hard
__ It's not spiritual having money
__ It's shameful being rich
__ Money can't buy love
__ Money causes problems
__ Money is hard to come by
__ Money is hard to deal with
__ Money is hard to get
__ Money is the root of all evil
__ Money slips through my hands

__ Money will change me for the worse
__ Never buy what you don't need
__ Only a select few get to have money
__ Poor people are more happy
__ Rich people are corrupt
__ Rich people are evil
__ Rich people are greedy
__ Rich people are stuck up
__ Rich people won't make it into heaven
__ I'm not good with money
__ Money causes stress
__ Money doesn't grow on trees
__ Money is a curse
__ Money is a pain in the neck
__ Money is dirty
__ Money is frustrating
__ Money only causes problems
__ You get what you deserve
__ I've never had money & never will
__ You have to struggle to survive
__ You have to suffer to get close to God
__ Rich people are just lucky
__ I'm going broke
__ I'm not allowed to have a lot of money
__ I'm only allowed to have enough
__ I'm not good enough to be rich
__ People who want money are shallow
__ Accepting money obligates me
__ Being rich is a sin
__ I am separate from money
__ I can never get ahead
__ I can't have money and free time
__ I can't handle having money
__ I don't work hard enough to have money
__ I can't save money

__ I do not have enough to share or give away
__ I don't deserve to have a lot of money
__ I don't know how to make money
__ Money makes me nervous
__ I give up when it comes to money
__ I hate money
__ I hate thinking about money
__ I do things I don't like to make money
__ I feel guilty for having money
__ I have to work so hard to make money
__ No matter what I do, I don't have enough money
__ People are mean to rich people
__ I really don't want money anyway

Do any of your answers surprise you? If you've really been honest with yourself, you should clearly see that with so many negative beliefs about money, it's amazing you have any money at all! But now, you are in a place to be able to change all of it. Awareness is the first step in setting yourself free. At the end of this book are positive affirmations you can start to repeat to yourself. It's time to re-affirm the commitment you made on the first day and to review your money goal. Find that note or 3x5 card where you wrote your Statement of Desire. Take a moment right now to read it aloud to yourself. Reaffirm the commitment you made on Day One.

Now, that you have made a firm decision to alter your money patterns once and for all, let's tap into what the *future* looks like when you have all that you desire. If you close your eyes and imagine waking up in a place and time where all your goals and dreams are fulfilled, where do you find yourself? Explore the environment. Do it in great detail. When you wake in the morning, what sounds do you hear? Do you hear the wind blowing through the trees? Do you hear the sound of ocean waves? Do you hear birds twittering outside your window? Perhaps you hear horses or cows. Or, perhaps you are living in a high rise in Manhattan and hear the buzzing traffic outside.

When you first open your eyes in the morning, what do you see around you? What colors are in the room? Soft whites and beiges? Vibrant blues and greens? Notice the windows and the types of curtains. Is there a sheer white curtain billowing in the morning breeze? Notice the light that comes in. Notice the furnishings around you. Who else is there with you? Do you hear voices down the hall or down the stairs? Feel the luxury of soft cotton or satin sheets. When you get out of bed, notice how the room is decorated. Notice the elegant furnishings. Notice the size of the room. Imagine that you walk to the bathroom and notice beautiful marble or expensive tile on the walls and floor. Touch the bath fixtures. Notice the details, the opulence.

Walk to your closet and notice the type of clothing you have, the quality of the fabrics. Are there layers of shelves for your shoes, for all your folded sweaters? Are there full length mirrors? These are the details of your new future where you are living in great opulence.

The intention in this exercise is to consciously decide what you want to have as a reality for your future. If you want to manifest more money, success is the result of this intention. Maybe success includes a photo of you in your dream BMW or driving a Lamborghini. If you want to manifest a new home, decide on the kind of home you want to manifest. Spend the rest of your day, fantasizing about your ideal future where you have billions of dollars. Focus on what you do want, not what you don't want. Use the exercises below to assist you in detailing this amazing, opulent ideal day in your future.

EXERCISE 5

IMAGINING YOUR IDEAL DAY

In this exercise, you are going to further enhance your goal for great wealth. What goal did you write in your Statement of Desire that you are reading twice a day? With that goal in mind, close your eyes and imagine that you wake up in the morning in your ideal future where you have already accomplished this goal. Using the lines below, answer the following questions:

1. When you wake up in the new future, where are you? Describe the room in detail? What color are the walls, the floors and the furnishings. What sounds do you hear? When you look out the window, what do you see, i.e. green rolling hills, horses in pasture? Mountains? The beach? High rise buildings?

2. Describe the kind of furnishings you see. What kind of bed are you in? What color are the sheets? What size is the room? Is there a fireplace in the room, chairs, a sofa, a television?

3. Imagine you get out of bed and walk across the room. Notice the carpet, the flooring, the rugs. Feel how soft and rich they feel. Walk into the bathroom and see it in detail: the size of the room, the cabinets, the fixtures? Write down what you see.

4. Now, walk into your closet and describe the size of it, the color of the cabinets in the closet and the clothing that you see. You are a multi-millionaire and have very expensive clothes. Describe the clothing in detail. Perhaps you see a pair of silk trousers or a beaded evening gown or Italian designer shoes?

DAY 6

YOUR MONEY MATRIX

As you are discovering beliefs about money, you should be getting a better idea of why money has been an obstacle for you or, at the very least, why you have not been able to create more money in your life. In this section, we will be going deeper into the beliefs you hold about money, beliefs you learned as a child.

Just as you know that you are the creator of your reality, so are you the creator of the money you allow in and out of your life. It may seem like bad luck that you lost your job or that the company you were working for went out of business, but it is all coming from you. In your childhood, you were taught all kinds of things about love, about life, and even about who you are. Included in those messages are the ones you received about money and what it means to be rich or to be poor. In essence, you developed beliefs about money that when all wired together create a matrix that holds your money reality in place. We're going to explore this matrix so you can take it apart and rebuild it into what you want it to be.

As a child, you learned about money based on how your parents handled money, how they talked about money, how they related to each other regarding money, and based on your own experiences with money.

DAY 6

Each of the things you heard, saw, and experienced, blended together into a personal money pattern. In fact, it is more than a pattern, it is a matrix that is twisted and bound together and operates very beautifully to create what you currently experience about money. To understand your matrix and take it apart, it becomes important to understand what you learned about money as you were growing up.

- Did you grow up in a *comfortable* home?
- Did your parents struggle for money?
- Did your parents fight about money?
- Did your mother or father tell you that money is dirty?
- Were you told that people who have money are unhappy? Selfish? Evil?

What messages did you get about earning money, about receiving money, and about how much you are allowed to have? Write down what you remember in your notebook following the exercises below. These beliefs form the walls, ceiling, and floor of your money matrix.

So, what is a matrix? Merriam-Webster defines matrix as follows:

> *A situation or surrounding substance within which some-thing else originates, develops, or grows, e.g. the womb.*

Based on the above definition, you can see that a matrix is like a womb, a place where beliefs once seeded can grow and when they grow, take on a life of their own. The seeds that were planted in you as a child about money have grown and taken on their own form. They are invisible throughout your life. Have you ever wondered why some people make money effortlessly and why others, more likely you, are constantly in need of more or just on the edge of having enough? People who are wealthy don't always come from abundant childhoods. You often hear stories of "self-made millionaires" or how someone rose "from rags to riches." What is common to these people, even those who struggled from poverty - is the *burning desire* that we spoke of previously. That *desire* is fueled by beliefs that are quite different from poverty stricken people. According to Steve Siebold, rich people think completely differently than poor people or even middle class people. Even those born in poverty who ultimately create great wealth do so because their beliefs about money and wealth are different than people who remain in poverty. Siebold states:

> *The secret [to wealth] is not in the mechanics of money, but in the level of thinking that generates it. Once you learn to embrace this, your earning potential is limitless.*[2]

Based on all of the messages you received as a child verbally, emotionally, and physically, you began to develop some very finite beliefs about money, wealth, and how it all works for you. In some instances, you were specifically taught how to handle money. For example, some parents teach their children by giving them a pretend check book allowing them to learn how to deposit monies and deduct what is spent (even if it is only play money.) One man, as a child, was taught that if he wanted to buy something he could borrow money from his father and then pay his father back in payments. Though his father thought he was teaching his son responsibility, forty years later, his son is still living in debt, making monthly payments. Another woman, who grew up in an abundant life style as a child, has spent her entire adulthood in debt, feeling powerless because she never learned how to earn her own money. If she ever needed money her father would give it to her, so as an adult she believes that she can only get money from someone else.

Most people never bother to determine what beliefs they have formed

---

[2] Siebold, Steve, How Rich People Think (2010) Sourcebooks, Inc.

DAY 6

over their lifetime. In most instances, the majority of beliefs are formed in childhood based on what you are told, what you heard and what you experienced. Over time, beliefs such as "rich people aren't happy" or "people who want money are selfish" are reinforced through experiences and, if not changed, ultimately become the reality you live. But, the belief was formed first. *Reality follows belief*, not the other way around. The matrix you have formed has become quite complex. It not only birthed many limiting beliefs about money, but it maintains those beliefs, protects them and keeps them in place. Therefore, if you want to change your experience of money and of wealth, this matrix needs to be taken apart. Let's do that now.

Take time today to write out everything you remember about your experiences with money as a child; what you were told, what you heard, what you experienced, what it means, and how you have incorporated those things into your life.

This matrix has been operating on automatic all of your life. Even though it may seem like fate is at work, it wasn't really the economy that created you losing your job or those extra taxes that put you in debt. You are creating your reality - all of it - and your money matrix is operating 24/7. Your subconscious diligently follows the dictates of the money matrix you have been forming all of your life.

EXERCISE 6

DISCOVER YOUR MONEY MATRIX

1. What do you recall being told about money when you were a child? Your answers can be things like, "Don't touch money. It's dirty." "Those rich people aren't happy." "Just get a job and a paycheck." Write as many things as you can remember about what you recall being told about money.

2. What did you learn from your parents about money based on how they handled money? In this section, write down what you remember about your parents' money habits. Did your mother complain often that she was worried about not having enough money? Did your parents fight about money? Was your father often absent because he "had to earn a living?" Were your parents liberal in how they handled and spent money? Were they conservative?

3. What do you remember about your own experiences involving money as a child? For example, did you receive an allowance? Were you taught to save your money so you could buy what you wanted or needed? If you asked for money, did your parents get angry? If you needed something, did you have to rely on someone else to buy it? Did you have to go without because there wasn't enough money?

4. What is your current money pattern? Taking in the information you wrote to the above questions how do you currently handle money? For example, you always have enough or, no matter what you do, you never have enough, or, you don't worry about it because you know if you get in trouble you will find help. Give this question a lot of thought because this is your current money thermostat.

DAY 7

YOUR EARNING PATTERN

If you did the exercises in the prior chapter, you should be getting a good idea of how your money matrix was formed and becoming aware of how it has been operating. As you look back on your life, what significant events involving money do you recall? When you got out of high school, did you get a job? Did you go to college? Did you have enough money to live as you wanted? Did you have to work to make ends meet? If you went to college, who paid your tuition? Who paid for your room and board and free time events? As you grew older, what kind of income did you earn? Did you take vacations and, if so, what kind of vacations did you take?

As you investigate these past incidents, you are adding more information to your understanding of your money matrix. This matrix is very powerful and important to understand. You learned a great deal about money from your parents or caregivers as you were growing up, but there is one parent we are going to discuss who is more significant than any other person in your life when it comes to understanding this matrix. That person is your father. Why is he so important to this issue? Your relationship with father or the *fathering* parent is important because your father is the parent you reach toward to *earn* love, attention, and

Day 7

affection. Though your mother is certainly significant in your early years, mother is usually the one who is there from the moment of your birth, tending to your needs without question. You are not required to ask or earn anything from her as she just provides it. In those very early years, father is often in the background, tending to your needs when mother asks for his help or when mother isn't available. Years later, however, getting father's attention becomes most significant. When you are about six or seven years old, as you begin to break away from the strong attachment you have held to your mother, you turn to father, seeking his approval and attention. How successful or unsuccessful you were in obtaining his love and attention; how successful you were in *earning* his affection - directly influences your relationship to money, *i.e.* your ability to *earn*.

Previously, you began identifying beliefs that are part of your money matrix, the fertile womb of beliefs within which you have been creating your reality around money. Now, we are going to delve deeper into this matrix, exploring your relationship with *earning*. How successful were you in *earning* your father's attention and love?

Was your father present, but not actively involved in your life? Was your father hot and cold in his relationship with you? Was your father absent from your life at an early age? Was your father not around at all due to death or divorce?

Now, compare the relationship you had with your father to your relationship with earning. If your father was around, but not involved in your life, then you probably have a pattern of having just enough money to cover your needs, but nothing more. If your father was in and out of your life, meaning he was sometimes there for you and other times not, then you probably have a pattern of money coming in and then disappearing only to come back again at a later time. If your relationship with your father was that you just couldn't win with him, no matter what you did, then your earning pattern is, no doubt, the same.

Now, you may be wondering how is *earning* different from other patterns you may have regarding money. Merriam-Webster defines earning much differently than "receiving":

1. *to gain or get in return for one's labor or service*
2. *to merit as compensation, as for service; deserve*
3. *to acquire through merit*
4. *to gain as due return or profit*
5. *to bring about or cause deservedly*

Take the time in the exercises that follow to write out what you remember about your relationship with your father from the time you were a little child all the way up to the present. How does your current money pattern compare to what you remember about your relationship with your father? What similar patterns do you notice? Allow yourself to delve into an understanding of your pattern of *earning* and how you played it out with your father.

EXERCISE 7
YOUR EARNING PATTERN

1. What do you recall with regard to your father being present in your life when you were a child?

2. What do you recall about your relationship with your father when you were 6-8 years of age? (This is the age when most children turn to father as a very significant parent in their life.)

3. Do you recall any incidents in particular in your childhood where your father was or was not available? Is so, describe them in detail.

4. Describe your ability (or inability) to earn money right now.

5. Compare your ability to earn money now to what you remember about your relationship with your father? What similar patterns do you notice?

6. Describe your money pattern as you currently experience it. Write it in first person, present tense. Here's an example:

> "I seem to always be struggling to have enough. I never seem to get ahead. As soon as it looks like I am going to get out of the hole I'm in, another bill comes in."
>
> Or
>
> "I have plenty of money as long as I get it from someone else. My husband supports me and pays all the bills, but I don't really have any of my own money."

7. Earning Meditation

Here is a meditation to help you see the pattern with your Father, the parent of earning, the parent for whom you performed in order to get their attention. Find a quiet space where you will be uninterrupted and follow these steps:

Allow yourself to relax, getting comfortable and closing your eyes when ready. Allow yourself to just let go and as you let go, just feel your body relax. Let whatever emotions you are feeling float by. Let them swirl and twirl and fall to the background. Allow all the thoughts and chatter in your conscious mind to fall to the background. Let your breathing relax you more, taking you to a deep state of relaxation. Letting go. And as you are letting go, just imagine that you are floating back in time. Feel yourself moving like a film on rewind and all the activity and movement begins to turn backwards. You move backwards, moving through your adult years, back through young adult years. Continue to move backwards, through space, back through time, moving through your teen years, then back through your childhood years coming to the time when as a child you first turned to focus your full attention on father. Perhaps he was always there, but you just noticed for the first time that this is someone who's attention you seek. You are about 6 or 7 years old. Go there now. Go to your childhood home and be that child.

Feel yourself in that child's body at around the age of 6 or 7. You are in first grade or perhaps second grade. You not only notice father, but you long for and want his attention. See yourself there now as this child, seeking father's love and attention. What do you notice? Is father not there? Is he always working, always struggling to make money? Has father left, abandoned the family? He died and left mother to handle all the bills, all the money; leaving mother to struggle to support you? Or, is father there, giving you just enough love and attention, but

MEDITATION

no more?

What do you learn about earning? How hard do you work for father's attention? Sense it. See it or feel it in the context of your money pattern. Do you always earn just enough and no more? Do you get lots and lots of love and attention and then it all stops? It is all taken away until the next time resulting in you creating a money pattern where you earn lots of money until it is all taken away. In and out, having lots and lots and then having none.

Is your relationship with father one of owing where you never feel you do enough; that no matter how hard you work you never get enough? Or, no matter how much attention and love father gives you, there are strings attached? You owe. You are in debt, constantly trying to pay back the little attention you get? What's your pattern of earning?

Do you learn that you have to take care of yourself because he's unreliable? You only get enough. If you work really, really hard, you might get a little bit. Or, is the relationship just not there at all? Father's gone. No matter how hard you work, you'll never get what you want?

Notice the pattern. Notice how you play it out in your day-to-day life with money. Just having enough or perhaps working so hard for little reward or getting lots and lots of attention only to have it bottom out to zero. Always struggling, striving to get what you want and never fully succeeding. Notice the pattern.

Sense the beliefs you have formed about earning and how you transform your childhood desires, successes, and failures into beliefs about earning; into beliefs about what you deserve.

Now, change the pattern with the power of your imagination. See that little boy or girl getting what they want. See them turning to father for father's love and attention and getting more than they ever imagined. Notice how this child reaches to father and father responds instantly showering this child with love, affection and attention. Feel yourself responding with delight, receiving the showering of love. Feel the shower of love just washing over you, pouring all over you. No matter what you do, no matter what you ask for, the slightest desire for father's attention is met with an overflowing response of incredible love and attention. Everything you do is met with his delight. He looks at you with adoration. You sing. You dance. You perform to his delight. There's no limit to the love you receive from this man. You earn more than enough. You earn all of his love, constantly and continuously. As you grow, your relationship of earning father's love continues to grow, to expand through your teen years, through your adult years. Father taught you all about money, about being rich, about seeking opportunities to excel and perform using your innate talents and skills.

Feel your heart fill with pride and joy and delight. This relationship with father is a foundation of your ability to earn and you earn without limitation. Your earning ability is equal to the amount of overflowing love you receive from this relationship with father. Consistent, flowing. Bountiful. Feel how good it feels. Feel how powerful you are.

Empowered with the ability to take action on that power; creating a life that's filled with success, continually striving and achieving, reaching for the stars and winning.

Allow yourself to move forward in time once again, traveling through all the years of your life with this new foundation of earning and as you come back to the present, feel your heart full of love and knowing you can have anything you want. Sense how you are healing all the beliefs you have held about yourself and about earning and your ability to receive. Feel that the limiting beliefs have shifted and changed. You are open to the bounty and abundance, the prosperity that is available to you without limit. Carry this feeling with you continuously throughout the day, throughout the weeks, months and years ahead. Sense how it changes your ability to earn money with the

MEDITATION

same sense of success, achievement that you have now.

Now, allow yourself to come back into your body, opening your eyes at the count of five. Coming back now: one, two, three four and five. Open your eyes. Come fully back knowing you have altered your pattern of earning.

[Go to www.annesayers.com to purchase downloadable meditations and recorded visualizations to augment what you are learning in this book.]

DAY 8

CHANGING BELIEFS

We all know how important beliefs are. There is no doubt that having the ability to take charge of your beliefs, consciously selecting which ones to keep and which ones to discard, is a powerful talent that can change your life. There are numerous belief changing techniques and all can be effective. What is important is finding one that works best for you. The first step is to discover what beliefs are holding you back and determining what beliefs you want to put in their place. You should have already discovered limiting beliefs about money that have been in place and should be in the process of building a nice list of empowering beliefs that you want to keep. If you haven't already done so, read the list of *Beliefs that Rich People Hold* at the end of this book. When you do so you will probably discover some empowering beliefs to add to your list. But, how do you determine what beliefs you want to release? Sometimes making this determination can be difficult.

In this section, we are going to delve more deeply into the limiting beliefs that are holding you back. As you know, beliefs are instructions to your subconscious of what you want to manifest in your life. If you have a belief, for example, that "nothing ever works for me," your subconscious will operate on that instruction making sure that "nothing

DAY 8

ever works for you!" Clearly, that is a belief you want to change.

Some limiting beliefs are easy to find. You may hear yourself saying the phrase "nothing ever works for me." Clearly, that is one that you want to write down. You may know that you have a fear around having money or that you believe you must struggle before you can get what you want. A great idea is to keep a little book in your pocket or purse so you can start writing down every belief you discover you hold around money and wealth. As you pay attention to what you say and think throughout your day, you will discover more and more beliefs. Keep writing them down. You have literally hundreds of thousands of beliefs and are continually making new ones all the time. Many of these beliefs are valuable and important and are beliefs you want to keep, but, you may also find constricting beliefs that are operating in your daily life of which you were never before aware.

For example, perhaps you are a person who has always struggled with your weight. You may know you hold a belief that "losing weight is a struggle," but what you may NOT know is that you also have a belief that "big people are more powerful than small people." Perhaps, you also hold a supporting belief that "people who aren't powerful get hurt." These are, obviously, important beliefs to discover as your desire to *lose* weight directly contradicts the beliefs you hold about power. If power and ultimately keeping yourself safe are more important than losing weight, you are not going to EVER lose weight.

Making money is the same. If you hold a belief that other people resent those who have a lot of money and you want to be liked, obviously, the desire to be liked will prevent you from making a lot of money. In the exercises that follow, you will have an opportunity to discover more about the subtle and often hidden beliefs you hold. You will also be given some great tools for altering beliefs.

The best scale for discovering beliefs is to look at your physical reality. Everything you have and don't have is a reflection of your beliefs.

Your subconscious is creating everything in your reality from the instructions you are giving it. To change your reality, therefore, you need to discover and alter these instructions, *i.e.*, beliefs. Start by writing a short biography of your life. Begin with the sentence "My life right now is _____." Then continue to write out everything you observe around you. Here's a sample:

My life right now is just okay. I have enough things, but I am not getting what I really want. I find myself scared most of the time to step beyond what I currently have. I have a job that is just okay, but it isn't what I really want to do. I am afraid to quit because that is the only way I know to make money.

Or,

My life right now is great. I have been pursuing my dream for some time now and I am excited about the potential, but it seems that I am always in the same place. I want to have more, but it is still a struggle. No matter what I do, I have to work so hard and nothing changes."

As you can see from these two examples writing out your current situation gives a lot of clues about what beliefs you have. After you write out your current bio, start making a list of questions and beliefs that you are seeing or sensing. In the first example, you may ask, "*Why is my life just okay?*" What more do you want that would make it more than just "okay?" Then ask yourself what is stopping you from having those additional things that you want. Even if it is, "people don't seem to recognize my talents" or "opportunities slip through my fingers", those are beliefs, or clues to beliefs, that you can write down in your little book of beliefs. Make a list of as many things you can think of that may be limiting you based on what you wrote. Notice particular words that you wrote such as "I can't", "he won't", "it's not", "I have to", "you should", "he

DAY 8

must." Note any places where you have written generalized statements such as "I always", "it never", "everything is" as well as words that may show where you rationalize things such as "because", "forced", "makes me" "let's me", etc.

You can also go to the pages on *Money Beliefs* or *How Rich People Think* at the end of this book and start circling additional beliefs that you know apply to you. After you have written down as many beliefs you can find, circle those that seem to be the most limiting. Those should be the first ones you set out to change.

Now, here's the fun part. You can CHANGE ANY BELIEF! No matter how huge it may appear in your life, no matter how challenging a belief may be, it is *just* a belief and any belief can be changed. How do you do it? There are some really great techniques out there, but the goal in each is to give a very clear message to your subconscious that you want to change, delete, or even destroy the old belief and replace it with a new one. Here are some suggestions:

1. **Xing Beliefs:** Write out the belief, or beliefs, that you want to change on a sheet of paper and then actively let your subconscious know that you no longer want this belief by Xing through it and, ultimately ripping up the paper, and destroying it.

2. **Seeing a Belief Differently:** Change the way you see or sense the belief or how the belief plays out in your life by "seeing" it in the same way that you see positive, powerful beliefs.

3. **Changing Technique**: Imagine that each belief is a garment of clothing that you can put on and take off at will. When you find one that you no longer want, take it off and throw it into a fire or incinerator until it is completely destroyed.

In the exercises that follow, write out what you are discovering about the beliefs you hold about money. Review the list of beliefs you have written and mark those you want to change. Then use any of the belief changing techniques described previously or others you may know or find to begin to alter the beliefs you have been holding and replace them with new and empowering ones.

EXERCISE 8

DISCOVERING & CHANGING BELIEFS

FINDING AND IDENTIFYING BELIEFS:

1. Identifying beliefs is sometimes like solving a mystery. You have to follow clues to get down to the hidden beliefs. In this exercise, write out a paragraph that describes your present life starting with a sentence such as "my money situation right now is _____." Write for as long as you feel the need, whether that be several paragraphs or several pages.

2. After a few hours, go back and read what you wrote above. Analyze it, looking for beliefs. Look for key words that may indicate a belief is there. Notice and circle particular words that you wrote such as "I can't", "he won't", "it's not", "I have to", "you should", "he must." Note any places where you have written generalized statements such as "I always", "everything is" "it never", as well as clue words that may show where you rationalize things such as "because", "forced", "makes", etc. Write out what you discover in your journal.

3. Review the list of beliefs you have written from the exercise above, including those that you have written in prior exercises. Circle the ones you deem are most important and that you want to change now. Then write them down in the order you deem most important. Choose from any of the options below to change the beliefs you no longer want to have.

OPTION I. Destroy unwanted beliefs:

Write out the belief you want to change on a blank sheet of paper. Next, take a large magic marker in any color and put a huge "X" through the entire phrase that you have written. Fold the paper up and set it aside for a few hours or until the next day. In your notebook or journal, write down the belief you wrote down and why you want to change it. Put as much emotion as possible into your writing!

After waiting a few hours or until the next day, open up the paper with the X'd out belief and read it again to yourself. Now, summon up as much emotion as you can and crumple up the paper yelling "No! "No! "No!" Then rip the paper into pieces with gusto and throw it into the fireplace, or into a fireproof bucket or in the sink. Set it on fire and watch it burn. If ashes remain, pulverize the ashes and throw them to the wind or put them in the trash, sensing that this belief is no more. In your notebook, write out how good it feels to be free of that belief.

New *Belief:* Next, write out the positive belief that is the opposite of the belief you just destroyed that will replace the prior belief. With the same amount of gusto, read it aloud and yell "Yes, Yes, Yes!" Imagine that you are embracing this new belief with both arms and pulling it into your heart. Again, use as much emotion as you can.

OPTION II. Alter How You See or Sense a Belief:
Discover how you "see", "sense", "feel", etc. the limited or constricting belief that you want to end. For example, if you have a belief that: "People don't like me," close your eyes and sense how you know this is untrue. What do you see? Sense? Feel? Write down the specifics of how you know this belief is untrue. Include any physical and emotional sensations.

Discover how you "see", "sense", "feel", etc. any positive belief that you currently hold. For example, if you have a belief: "I am really good at my job," close your eyes and sense how you know this is true. Do you see something, feel something? Write down the specifics of how you know it is true and include any physical and emotional sensations that express how good it feels.

EXERCISE 8

Compare how you sense/experience these two opposite beliefs. For example, if it is an image, where is it in your mind's eye? Is it high or low? What color is it? How large or small? Is it heavy or light? Write down the details of these differences and then write out how the limiting belief is different from the positive one.

Now, install the belief that you want to have. Remembering the details of the positive belief above, create this new belief in exactly the same way. See it, sense it, feel it exactly the same as you felt the positive belief you first identified. If the positive belief is an image that is close up, a little to your right and very bright and clear, then do the same for the new belief you want to implant. Write on the lines below what you experience.

Lastly, take the belief you want to release and do just the opposite - *i.e.*, push it out far away, place the image up high and to the left. Make it very fuzzy and unclear. How does that feel? Repeat the exercise until you feel the belief is altered.

OPTION III: Belief Changing Room:

In this exercise, imagine that your beliefs are clothing that you wear. Close your eyes and begin to sense a limiting belief. Feel how it feels and as you are doing this, imagine you are wearing the belief. Sense the belief you are wearing. Is it heavy or light? Is it soft to the touch? Smooth? Rough? Silky? Imagine you look at yourself in a mirror. See what this garment/belief looks like. What color is it? What is the style? How long or short is it? How does it feel? Is it something you designed and created or something that someone gave to you? Imagine you remove the garment. Thank it for serving you so well. Imagine you are standing near a burning campfire. Throw the garment into the campfire watching it burn until it is completely destroyed. There is nothing left of it - not even ash.

Next, imagine the belief you want to have. Close your eyes and feel the new belief. How does it feel to be happy? Successful? Loved? Open your eyes and look in the mirror once again, this time seeing a new garment that expresses these new, positive feelings. Feel how good it feels to be wearing it. Write out your experiences in your journal or notebook.

Now, go back and read what you wrote, analyzing it for beliefs. As discussed above, look for key words and if you think there is a belief behind it, write it down in your journal or notebook. You can always come back and add, delete, or change anything you have written.

Review the list of beliefs you have written down including those from prior exercises. Select those you want to change now. Then use any of the belief changing techniques described above to alter the beliefs you have been holding for years.

Meditation: Changing Room Technique

Allow yourself to get relaxed and when you are ready close your eyes finding that comfortable place. Let go of all thoughts and feelings. Put your focus on each breath, noticing the rise and fall of each inhale and exhale. Begin to slow down each breath with a longer inhale and longer exhale.

Imagine you are descending a staircase that is taking you to the realm of your subconscious. It might be a spiral staircase, or a wooden one or a beautiful, elaborate marble staircase. Imagine yourself descending the stairs heading toward your subconscious. Feel each foot step down lower as each leg bends. If you come to a landing, walk across the landing to the next set of steps and descend once more. Feel yourself going deeper with each step as you head to the realm of your subconscious to a belief changing room.

Step off the last step at the bottom of this tall staircase. You are standing in front of an entry door that says "Subconscious Mind" in bold letters. Pull the door open and step through the doorway, finding

EXERCISE 8

yourself inside the realm of your subconscious. You are seeking a room of beliefs - a changing room. You begin to walk down the corridor. Perhaps you find yourself in a dark warehouse, with high ceilings, dusty crates and boxes of things that are stored here. Smell the dust. Hear your footsteps as you walk. Perhaps you are in a huge library with thousands of books stacked high, wall to wall. Perhaps you are in a computer center and you can hear the hum of the giant computers with lights flickering. Walk through this corridor. You will be passing rooms with closed doors looking for the room of changing beliefs.

Continue to walk and up ahead you see a room that looks familiar. On the outside of the door it says "Changing Room." Try the door knob to see if it is locked. If it is unlocked, imagine you turn the latch and the door opens. If the door is locked, imagine you have a key in your pocket or on a chain around your neck. Take out the key and unlatch the lock. Gently sense the door opening. You walk into a dimly lit room. Inside the room, there is a giant 3-way mirror. You can see yourself on multiple sides. This is the room for changing beliefs. Stand here in front of the changing mirror and close your eyes.

Start thinking about the belief you want to change. Perhaps it's a belief that "I'm not enough" or a belief that "I don't deserve" or a belief that "I have to suffer or struggle to have money." Get a sense of the belief. Think about it and all the consequences you have suffered as a result of this belief. How does it feel?

Feel the weight of it. Imagine that this belief is a piece of cloth draped across your body. Feel the texture of the fabric. Is it soft? Rough? Then open your eyes and see what you are wearing. Perhaps it smells old and dusty. Is it a garment that goes to the floor? Perhaps it is colorful and childlike. Was it something given to you? Is it a costume? Notice the detail. What does it feel like to wear this belief? As you look at it, make a decision that you want to discard this belief so that you can find a new one.

Create a new belief that you can wear from this day forward. As you make this decision, unsnap the snaps on the garment; undo the buttons. If it has a zipper, unzip it or simply slip it off your arms, let it drop to the floor, or pull it over your head. Hold this belief in your arms. Was this a belief you created? Was it a belief that was given to you? Thank this belief for serving you all these years. Then take the garment and put it in a discard pile.

Looking into the mirror, start thinking of what belief you want to put in its place. Perhaps a belief that "I deserve," "I am worthy," that I am "powerful and majestic;" a belief that "I am bountiful and wealthy." Whatever the new belief it, close your eyes and imagine once again that you are feeling this belief materializing as a garment across your body. Perhaps you feel the weight across your shoulders or do you feel the silkiness as it flows down your body? Touch it with your hands. This belief is new. Is it soft, light? Sparkly?

Open your eyes and look in the mirror and see yourself in the new garment. Notice the beautiful details. Mostly, notice how you feel as you look in the mirror wearing this beautiful new garment. Feel how magnificent it feels to be wearing this new belief.

Now, wearing your new garment, pick up the discarded one. Holding the discarded belief in your arms, open the door and walk back to the corridor. In the distance, see an incinerator burning brightly in the dim light. Walk down the corridor to the incinerator. Once again, thank the old belief for serving you all these years. Open the incinerator and throw the old garment into the flames. Watch it burn. Perhaps it bursts into flames. Perhaps it gives off a dark smoke. Watch it burn and slowly disintegrate as the fire eats away at the garment, turning it into ash. Watch as even the ash disintegrates ash so there is nothing left. When it is completely gone, close the door to the incinerator and walk back down the corridor.

You can return to the changing room and try on new beliefs just like

EXERCISE 8

you try on new clothing or you can leave the realm of the subconscious to come back another day to change any other belief you desire to change.

Allow yourself to come back now into the room where you started. Feel yourself changed now that an old belief has been removed and incinerated and a new belief is now a part of you. Feel that it is changed. Feel that you are changed.

Sense the room around you. Allow your breathing to go back to normal and at the count of five open your eyes: One, Two, Three, Four and Five.

While the memory is still fresh in your mind, write in your journal all that you experienced in the meditation. [And don't forget you can order these recorded meditations and visualizations from our site at www.annesayers.com.]

DAY 9

POWER OF THE SUBCONSCIOUS

You are already aware of how important the subconscious is. For many years it was thought that the subconscious was only a receiver of information, but it is now known that it is not only receiving billions of bits of data every minute, but it is translating, storing, and converting that data. The subconscious is the basis of all the work you do and have done to heal your past and to change your life. It is the subconscious that is holding all the beliefs you have formed, and it is keeping those beliefs in place. It is also the subconscious that is converting those beliefs into a manifested reality. Therefore, it is critically important that the subconscious cooperate with your new program of creating incredible wealth!

As discussed previously, you have a *money matrix* that you developed in childhood and which, like a thermostat, holds your money program in place. This matrix not only includes the issues you have around money and earning, but also the monetary ceiling that you cannot exceed. If, for example, your *pattern* says that you are only allowed to have $4000 a month in income and next month you exceed that amount, say $6000, then the month after, you will suddenly have unforeseen expenses, probably $2000 worth that get you back to your *norm*. If you did the

DAY 9

meditation at the end of Chapter 7, designed to alter your *earning* relationship, then you have given your subconscious a new message which is that you want to be unlimited in your ability to earn and to receive. Repeat that meditation as often as possible.

You have also started creating a new resonance of expanded bounty and prosperity. Everything we are doing here every day is to continue building this resonance; a resonance of how it feels to have already achieved great wealth; how it feels to have achieved what you wrote in your Statement of Desire on the first day. Your subconscious is *listening!* As you know, the subconscious will accept any messages you give to it. The challenge is how to get it to take in the right messages.

There are numerous techniques and processes available to do this, such as visualizations, meditations, even affirmations can be effective. The work you are doing is already getting the message through to your subconscious that you are altering and expanding your money image, but as you proceed with this program, resistances will start to come up. Be aware and ready to address any such resistances so you can continue on your way to creating the financial success you desire.

How do you know there are resistances coming up to your new programming of great wealth? Most often it will show up as fear or perhaps anger. You might experience meeting or coming in contact with wealthy people who are obnoxious, rude, and not the kind of people you want to emulate. Your reality is showing signs of resistance in the form of increased utility bills, a new tax notice, or some threat of harm.

Remember, you have previously given your subconscious strong messages about what you are allowed to have financially as well as emotionally and unless you change the programming, your subconscious will effectively work to keep you in the same place. To avert any potential of sabotaging your work thus far, make sure you do the meditation at the end of the prior chapter that is designed to alter old beliefs as well as to alter your *earning* pattern.

Here's some additional methods for reprogramming your subconscious:

- Meditate or visualize using music that evokes a lot of emotion while planting the message of what you want to create. Your subconscious responds strongly to emotions and pictures
- Handwrite a letter to your subconscious telling it exactly what you want (Write it in detail with as much emotion as possible)
- Close your eyes and carry on a dialogue with your subconscious making an agreement with it of what you want to create
- Repeat the meditation for "Belief Changing Room" described above in Chapter 8

Also, remember that when Jim Carrey visualized a check for $1 million dollars to himself for "acting services rendered", he also wrote a check to himself for that amount and carried it in his wallet for years until it actually happened. You can do any of these things. Find the one that works the best for you.

EXERCISE 9
REPROGRAMMING YOUR SUBCONSCIOUS

I. Write a Letter to Your Subconscious:

In this exercise, we're going to work with some additional methods for reprogramming your subconscious. The first one is to write a detailed letter to your subconscious, telling it about your desire to have great riches and the resistances you have been discovering. Ask it whatever it is you want to know including why you have the resistances you have. Write as though you are writing to a good friend who is a great ally and you must help them to clearly understand what it is you want. Make your language as direct as possible with "I wants" and not "I don't wants." When you finish writing, fold it up and stick it away for a while. You may have to write more than one letter. Keep repeating what it is you want. Write out what you experience in your notebook.

II. Write a Response Letter:

After you have gotten your point across clearly and have covered all of your questions, write a response letter. Pretend that you are your subconscious and answer all of the questions you wrote in your prior letter. Don't censor or limit the communication. Just write answers as you sense them. Let the words flow. Make sure you address every question in your original letter and give reasons why the patterns have remained or aren't changing. Continue this dialogue until you feel you have all the answers to your questions. When complete, write what you experienced in your notebook.

III. Write a final demand letter.

As you continue the dialogue with your subconscious, asking it questions and then writing the answers, you should have a much better understanding of not only the beliefs you formed, but why they are there. In this last exercise, give your subconscious direct instructions about what you now want in your life. Remember, your subconscious is like a computer. You cannot hurt its feelings. It has no emotions. It is strictly operating on the instructions it has received. Therefore, be as forceful as necessary to get your point across with as much emotion as possible because that is one of the ways that your subconscious got the old instructions in the first place. More than likely, in a moment of great pain or hurt or anger, you gave it instructions of what you "don't" deserve or what you do not want to have. Your subconscious has just been a good friend to you all these years – following those very old and now obsolete instructions. This final letter is an opportunity for you to instruct your subconscious that you want it to eliminate all limiting beliefs (be specific) and that you want to create, manifest and receive all the money that you set in your Statement of Desire. Write it with feeling and intent! Here's some guidelines to assist you in writing your letters:

Get details. Dialogue with your subconscious asking it the purpose of the resistance in detail. For example, it is not enough to just know that you are afraid of being rich. You want to know all the details of why that fear is there.

Make a commitment. Set an intention to work with your subconscious to find a solution. In other words, make a commitment to work together (not work against it.)

Find examples. Give your subconscious examples of people who have succeeded doing what it is you desire. Let your subconscious know that what you desire is possible. Understand your subconscious will do anything that you tell it is possible and the more examples you give it, the more it will be receptive.

EXERCISE 9

Solidify and affirm. Create a phrase that is a reminder of what it is you want and repeat it numerous times throughout your day. Particularly, repeat it just before you go to sleep and just as you wake in the morning or right after meditation when your subconscious is most available.

DAY 10
BUILDING RESONANCE

It's exciting to discover your money pattern. It should be making sense to you where you learned your pattern of earning and how it has been working all of your life. Now, that you have healed past relationships, you can get back to building the resonance of what you want to create. Are you still reading your Statement of Desire that you wrote on Day One? If not, get back to it. It is important that you not only know what that statement is, but that you have written it down and review it daily. Why? Because you need a roadmap of where you are going. It is a positive reminder to your subconscious of what you want to accomplish. The more information you give to your subconscious, the clearer the outcome becomes. The more precise the outcome, the more efficient the subconscious mind can become.

Have you ever taken a long trip by car? Can you imagine traveling across country without a written map? You could say that you don't need it because you know where you are going, but you also know that if you do that, you will never reach your destination.

You have written down your primary money goal which is your Statement of Desire. You've begun to imagine what you are going to do

DAY 10

with the money you have set as your goal. Perhaps you have imagined paying off all your credit card debt, paying off your car, or even paying off your mortgage. Perhaps you are going to buy a new car, take a trip to an exotic country, or even buy a new house. It is so important that you reinforce these dreams daily and this is how you are going to do it:

1. Imagine accomplishing the goal you have written in your Statement of Desire. Let's say your goal is to have "$1,000,000 within the year." Can you imagine how you will feel a year from now when you have $1,000,000 in your bank account? Close your eyes and feel how great that feels. Talk to yourself, saying things such as: "I am a millionaire!" "I did it!" "I am rich." "I am free from all my prior restrictions." "I created a million dollars." "If I can do this, I can do anything!"

2. Now, get in touch with how you are feeling physically in your body as you feel the reality of being a true millionaire. As you say the words "I am a millionaire," what do you feel physically in your body? Perhaps you feel your heart open. Perhaps you feel a stirring in your solar plexus. Notice everything about your body language as you say the words "I am a millionaire." How do you stand? What is your posture? How do you hold your hands? What kind of expression do you have on your face? These things are important to remember so that you can easily get into this state again and again every day.

3. Next, start adding things to your dream such as the new car that you have bought. Still standing tall, feeling your heart open, or your solar plexus stirring, imagine you are standing in front of your new car (or new house or new boat) looking at it. What color is it? How does it feel as you stand here looking at YOUR new car? Feel this in your body, the same way as described in number two above, feeling how great it feels to have your dream car. You are a millionaire! You just bought your dream car!

Get inside the car, smell the *new car smell*. Feel the leather dashboard. Feel the leather seats. Then turn on the engine and listen to it hum. This is your car. You are a millionaire driving your dream car. Feel the joy! Feel the thrill!

Each day repeat the above exercises so that you are continually building the resonance of who you are as a millionaire with your brand-new Lamborghini, or Mercedes, or BMW.

As you go throughout your day, whatever that may entail, keep reminding yourself that you are a millionaire with a brand-new luxury car or whatever it is that represents wealth to you. Use reminders throughout the day, such as seeing your dream car in the parking lot, or pretending that the car you are driving is the car of your dreams. The whole idea is to continually build your resonance on the *wealth* frequency that you are creating through the above exercises.

End this chapter by writing yourself a letter of what it feels like to receive the money you set as your goal in your Statement of Desire. Imagine all the events that led up to accomplishing your goal. Write it as though it has already happened or is happening now so that it stirs powerful feelings to carry with you throughout your day.

EXERCISE 10

YOUR MONEY LETTER

I. Write Yourself a Letter Describing Your New Life.

Write yourself a letter of what it feels like receiving the money you set as your goal in your Statement of Desire. Imagine the events and feelings that have lead up to accomplishing your goal. Write it as though it has already happened or is happening now so that it stirs the same feelings you imagined when you started this program. You don't have to figure out how it will happen. Just let it write itself and allow yourself to expand the feelings of how great it is to accomplish your goal! Here's an example of how that can be written.

> *I just received another check in my mail box and this one is even larger than the one I received last week. I never thought I would have this kind of money, but when I total up all of the checks I see that I am only $150,000 short of my goal of $1,000,000. I set this amount as a goal one year ago and even though I was feeling it as true, I am still amazed at the success I have created! And, it's not over yet. I still have money coming in! At this point, it appears that I am going to exceed my initial goal! Can you believe it? I set a goal a year ago of $1,000,000 and I did it! In fact, I created more than that and I know how I did it. My life will never be the same because I have changed so much. I not only have created the abundance that I always desired, but I feel like a millionaire and that is why I know this is who I will always be from now on.*

As you write your letter, let your imagination open and allow the words to flow.

DAY 11

RESISTANCES

Congratulations! You are now 11 days in to this resonance building program. If you've been working with it daily, you are doing the following steps each day:

1. Reading your Statement of Desire
2. Focusing on specific things you will do (and get) when you have all the money you have set as your goal
3. Building resonance by expanding and adding details to your goals, such as shopping real estate, reading about investment opportunities, test driving the type of car you will be buying. In other words, act *as if* you already have the money in hand
4. Doing specific things that *rich* people do such as going to the race track, going out to a fine restaurant or watching a polo game

And, now add a fifth thing:

Reread the letter you wrote yesterday about how it feels to have ALL the things you desire.

DAY 11

All of the above, along with visualizations and affirmations in each chapter, are done with the goal of altering the beliefs that have kept you where you have been financially. As you proceed each day, your subconscious is listening and responding and eventually will get the message that you want to expand your financial reality.

But, as you know, you formed a lot of beliefs over the years about money, how much you are allowed to have and what you have to do to get it. You are stretching your reality through a new resonance. The old beliefs are going to be triggered. That's okay. That means the exercises are working and you are stretching beyond the familiar, but you also need to address the fear and anxiety that may start to show itself. In addition to the above, we will be addressing how to process through the fears so you can reach a new level.

We've already discussed techniques for working with the subconscious. You've received a powerful meditation for releasing subconscious beliefs. In this section, we're going to add some additional techniques to move beyond anxiety or fears that may be building. What beliefs may stop your progress? How about a belief that "wealthy people are bad people" or "I don't deserve to be happy" or "I'm not allowed to have a lot of money." Whether you have identified the specific beliefs or not, any anxiety that you may be feeling is an indication that a resistance is building. That anxiety makes it difficult to hold the resonance that you have been working on for the last 10 days. It is also risky because if your old money pattern is still in place or if you have memories of being punished or humiliated for reaching for something you want, each day of resonance building can become more frightening. The good news, though, is that if you release the past incidents that are holding the old pattern in place, you can get right back to your resonance building, increasing your ability to manifest the wealth you desire.

The following process is an effective and powerful one for releasing conflicting and limiting beliefs and breaking old patterns. Follow the steps and see how good you feel when you are done!

IMPRINTING:

Imprinting is the process of forming foundational beliefs as the result of significant events from your past. In baby ducks, it has been observed that the idea of "mother" is imprinted early on based on the first thing they see right after they hatch. Whether it is a tennis ball or a puppy or a person, the ducklings will follow that object or thing because the belief that this is mother has already been *imprinted*. Likewise, you have *imprints* from your past, events that deeply *imprinted* beliefs that have been preventing you from being able to move beyond a limited financial reality. You already know many techniques to alter beliefs, but the following process, entitled "Re-Imprinting" is a very successful process to alter beliefs and to release fear and anxiety that may be coming up as a result of your new programming.

There are a total of eight steps which you can implement by following the details below.

1. Identify the feelings you want to change.
2. Trace the feelings back in time to the earliest incident that is connected with these feelings. Recall the event in as much detail as possible.
3. What beliefs and conclusions did you form as a result of that event or events?
4. What was the intent of the person or persons involved in that incident?
5. What other resources or choices does that person need to handle the event differently, *e.g.* self-acceptance, self-forgiveness, compassion, understanding, etc.
6. Imagine you give this resource to that person and that they now

DAY 11

respond differently. Imagine them operating differently in the incident(s) and feel how good it now feels.

7. Now imagine that you step into the body of the other person or persons involved in the incident(s). Feel how they feel and act now with the new resource. Imagine them acting completely differently. Imagine how you are responding to them now that they are acting differently. Feel your emotions in this new experience imagining what it feels like to be in the different experience.
8. Notice that you now can form new beliefs as a result of the changed incident.

Write down everything you have discovered in your notebook or journal.

EXERCISE 11

RE-IMPRINTING SIGNIFICANT EVENTS

This exercise is an excellent one for releasing "imprints" from significant events in your past. You don't need to go into a meditative state, but can write the answers to each question in your journal.

1. Desired state. If you accomplish your goal that you wrote in your Statement of Desire, how will it look, feel, sound, etc.? Create an image or a sense of what your desired outcome will be and write out in detail what you see and sense. Be detailed. For example, if your Statement of Desire is to be a millionaire imagine or sense the "you" sitting in your BMW in front of your estate, or sense yourself on your yacht or sitting on the beach at your beachfront estate. Allow yourself to sense or see what your life will be like once you have reached this goal.

2. Present state. Once again, use sensory images to see and sense your current financial state and write out what you are sensing and feeling.

3. What's in the way. Think about where you are at currently and where you want to be. As you think about these two different options, what comes up as an obstacle to reaching the new outcome? What constricting or limiting feelings are coming up? How does it make you feel that you may fail? You may not know the specifics of what's in the way at this point, but you can make a list based on what you are thinking and feeling. What do you find yourself saying as you think or talk about increasing your wealth?

4. Trace back. Trace these emotions back in time to the first incident you can remember when you felt these feelings. Let yourself see/sense the prior event in detail answering the following questions:

EXERCISE 11

Where are you?

How old are you?

Who is present?

What do you see/ sense /hear?

What is happening?

What conclusions have you made as a result of the incident?

5. Beliefs. What beliefs did you form as a result of that incident? Look back and see if there are any other beliefs or ways this experience has affected you. Did you form any judgments about yourself as a result of the incident? If so, did the judgments come from you or did you pick up judgments from the other person(s)?

6. Intent. What is the other person's intent in this incident - meaning, do they really want to harm or hurt you? Are they well intentioned, but just really off base? Are they attempting to protect you? Protect themselves? If this person knew today the impact of that incident on you, would they be satisfied with that?

7. Resource. What resource or quality can you give to this person or persons so that the respond differently?

8. Imagine. Imagine that you give that resource or quality to the person or persons in that incident. How do they act differently having that resource? Notice the details. How do they look when they speak now? How do they say it? How do you respond? How do you feel? Write out how different you feel now with the new significance you have given to the prior incident:

9. New beliefs. What beliefs do you now form?

10. Running backwards. Now, imagine that you take the new feelings and the new beliefs and run them backwards through the whole time period – sprinkling these feelings and beliefs through every incident. Feel how amazingly good you feel with the new understandings. Feel the relief. If your past is now changed to reflect these new feelings and beliefs, how will your life be different?

Write out what you have discovered in your notebook or journal.

DAY 12

MAKING IT REAL

The subconscious doesn't know the difference between what is *"real"* and what is *"imagined."* As far as the subconscious is concerned, whatever you create that involves your physical senses (smell, taste, touch, hearing, and sight) is real. This is why it is so important to continue to build your resonance by "acting as if" what you want is already yours.

By this point, you should already have a good idea of your *money pattern* and how it has operated with money all of your life. This pattern was built out of beliefs formed in your growing up years that you are now changing. Following the exercises in this program, you can deactivate your original *money pattern* and replace it with one that is unlimited in nature. You are altering beliefs and reprogramming your subconscious and ultimately building a new frequency. Thus, anything that supports this process is important and encouraged.

What are some great ways to keep this new frequency operating, and continuously building and growing? Neuro-scientists have discovered that the brain responds to three very specific actions designed to bring about change.

DAY 12

These actions are:

1. Repetition of the new belief or new habit
2. Disconnection or withdrawal from the old belief or habit
3. Adding in as much emotion as possible

Every moment of every day, your body is communicating with your brain through neural pathways. Research shows that with every thought you are using and conditioning these neural pathways. It doesn't matter whether you are thinking about the past, present or future, with every thought, you are strengthening the neural pathways associated with whatever you are thinking about. These pathways are like mini-highways that are carrying information through electrochemical impulses. As years go by, the pathways become thicker and more deeply imbedded in the brain. By the time you are 25 years old, you are very set in the ways you react, respond, and do things. According to psychologist William James, "In most of us, by the age of thirty, the character has set like plaster, and will never soften again."[3]

Neuroscientists have discovered, however, that the brain is very flexible and these pathways can be changed through focus and attention. According to the latest studies, a new neuro-pathway can be created out of nothing if the desired activity is repeated often enough.

> *The number of repetitions required to build enough myelin sheath to make a new network work at an unconscious level is between 30-50 times. This means that any new skill, including all the components within the skill may need to be repeated up to 50 times before it is embedded in the neurological system.*[4]

---

[3] William James in his 1890 book *The Principles of Psychology*.

[4] Richard L. Bryck, PhD and Philip A. Fisher, PhD, "Training the Brain: Practical Applications of Neural Plasticity", Journal of Neuroscience, 2013

You have no doubt already experienced this when attempting to learn a new skill. Let's say you are learning how to play tennis and your instructor tells you that you need to keep your elbow up higher when you swing. Though your tendency may be to lower your elbow, through practice and repetition, you will repeat swinging over and over again with your elbow up until it becomes automatic to do it that way. What is really happening in the brain is that as you are focusing and concentrating on the new behavior, you are creating a new neural pathway and, as you can see from the above excerpt, to develop the new pathway, you need to repeat the new behavior at least 30-50 times before it will begin to happen automatically.

This repetition is important because you are not only developing a new pathway, but you are also erasing the old pathway which eventually disappears through lack of use.

> *We also need to be aware that the old connections are much stronger than the new connections, which is why it is so easy to fall back into old habits.*[5]

It is, therefore, very important to remember to maintain your focus and attention on the new behaviors you want to develop. You are reinforcing a consciousness of abundance and prosperity. You are practicing daily what it feels like to be wealthy and to think in a whole new way. Just like remembering to keep your elbow up, you are reminding yourself to *act as if* you are already wealthy. You are repeating new behaviors, new thoughts, and new beliefs that are all in alignment with your goal of manifesting great wealth. As you do this, you are not only re-programming your subconscious mind, but you are also developing new neural pathways in your brain. Just like playing tennis,

---

[5] *IBID.*

DAY 12

in time you won't have to focus on acting as if you are already wealthy because the new pathways make the new behavior nearly automatic, *i.e.,* a new habit. Repeating the new behaviors is both adding a new pathway and erasing the prior one. Thus, it is extremely important that you stick with the exercises and continue to repeat the affirmations, review your Statement of Desire, and continue to practice your new identity of being a successful, wealthy person. In the beginning, it may be challenging to remember all these new steps, but, in time, new neural pathways will be well-embedded and the new behaviors will no longer be new. They will be habit.

Also, remember to focus on how happy and excited you feel in this new state of abundance. These positive emotions set a state of resonance that is very powerful, reinforcing the rebuilding of new neural pathways in your brain. You may have already noticed that being excited, happy, and enthusiastic makes this whole process more enjoyable and a lot easier. It is a scientific fact that what you focus upon will expand and grow. All your old beliefs of struggle and lack became deeply imbedded because of experiences that were emotional ones, more than likely, very painful ones. In your programming and resonance building, you can build positive emotions of excitement, happiness, enthusiasm, and anticipation in the same way you embedded the old constricting ones. This book is designed to assist you to repeat your new beliefs and new habits so you can build new neural pathways to reinforce them. The key is to repeat the new behaviors consistently with as much emotion as possible while stopping or reducing the use of the old behaviors. When you do this you are accelerating the process. You are not only demonstrating that you are fully committed to your new goal, but you are enhancing the process. Your subconscious assists the brain in developing new pathways and your brain is assisting your subconscious to accept the new program.

Below is a list of techniques you can use to assist you in the process of building new neural pathways:

- Close your eyes and imagine you have already received the amount of money on your Statement of Desire. Bring in all your senses. See the check or the money or the bank statement; touch it, smell it, hear yourself talking about it to other people. Imagine you hear people congratulating you on your newfound wealth and, even taste what it is to be truly wealthy!

- Visualize stacks of money everywhere in your home, stuffed in closets, drawers, and cabinets. See money stuffed in the bathtub, the shower, even the oven and refrigerator. When you cook, you have to move the money around. When you drive your car, you have to roll the windows up so money doesn't fly out the windows. When you reach into your pockets you find stacks of papers bills. As always, use your senses of sight, smell, hearing, taste, and touch to add realness and feel what it feels like to have money absolutely everywhere!

- Find an old check book and start writing checks to pay off all your debt, then, total up the money you have. In other words, reconcile your bank account that is holding millions of dollars, deducting the payments you just made. Feel how great it feels to pay off these debts and to be debt free, because you have millions of dollars coming in every day.

- Find photographs of money, gold bars, bulging wallets, even of the house you are going to buy, the new car, the vacation you are going to take. Cut pictures out of magazines and paste them onto a board or calendar that you can hang on the wall and see throughout your day, reminding you of your new-found wealth.

DAY 12

- Start shopping for the items you plan to buy with your new millions. Drive around the neighborhood where you are going to buy your new house. Shop for real estate. Test drive your new car. Go to the mall and walk through Neiman Marcus or Saks 5th Avenue or Gucci or Prada. All the while, feel the excitement of owning all these new things.

- Circle of Abundance: create a circle filled with the energy of abundance. Get a large piece of paper or a carpet swatch that will be the core of your circle of abundance. Close your eyes and stand in front of this paper or carpet swatch, imagining that you are filling it with the energy of money. Imagine that this circle is filled with millions of dollars. Imagine that you are adding in the joy of what it feels like to have millions of dollars. Add in fun, happiness, and laughter. Then, open your eyes and count from one to three. When you get to the number three, step forward into the circle. Once again, close your eyes and feel how amazing it feels to have the resonance of all these energies flowing and circling around you. Imagine that your entire body is filling with this resonance of joy, abundance, bounty, happiness, and laughter. Don't step out of the circle until you are filled with these energies. Carry this with you the rest of your day and if you need a "refill", step into the circle again!

Three things to remember to enhance the resonance of bounty and abundance and to make the vision stronger and more real:

IMAGINE! FEEL! REPEAT!

Remember, to create the success you want, it is important to become the person who is already experiencing it. If you want more money adopt the mindset of a wealthy person. Be specific about your goal and then become the person who has that kind of wealth - in your mind, in your heart, in your vibration. Remind yourself by asking questions such as:

- How does a millionaire wake up in the morning?
- What would a millionaire order for lunch today?
- How does a millionaire walk?
- How does a millionaire talk on the phone?
- How do they sit, smile, shop, talk, listen, etc.?

Each time you ask these questions, answer by imagining that you are already a millionaire, sensing how a millionaire wakes up in the morning; how a millionaire walks and talks; mimicking that behavior throughout the entire day. Even though it may feel very different, you have to be that difference now. You are creating and developing new pathways in your brain and it will only happen through effort. Tune in every day to how you feel about being a millionaire; feeling good about who you are and what you do for a living.

Remember to practice the vibration of what it is you are manifesting and soon it will be real.

EXERCISE 12

EXERCISE 12

PRETENDING "AS IF"

1. How does it feel to look at the above bank receipt for $99 million dollars knowing that it is from YOUR personal savings account? Can you imagine it as yours? What do the little voices say in your head? "It's not possible!" "I don't believe it!" Be honest with yourself and write down every thought and feeling that comes up – both positive and negative. Get detailed about how it feels to have that kind of money in your savings account. As you imagine the above receipt is from your bank account, what emotions do you feel? Where do you feel it in your body? In your heart? In your solar plexus? What else do you feel physically? Describe it in detail and write it out in your journal.

MONEY MAGICALLY

Imagine that the following bank statement is from your personal checking account. Describe in your notebook how it feels to have over $6 million dollars in your bank account.

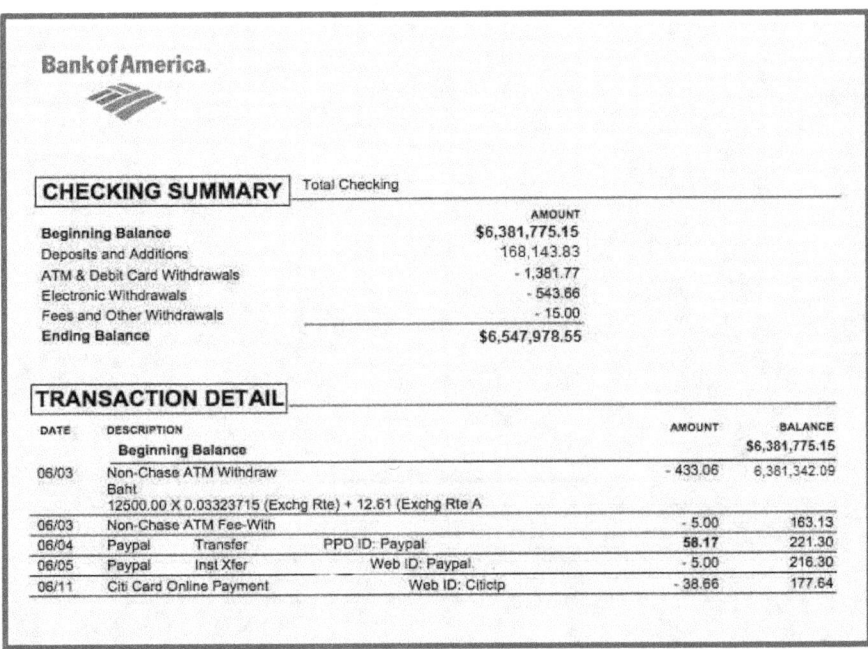

Add your name to the check below. How does it feel to receive a check for over $1 million?

DAY 13

SELF-IMAGE

Self-image is one of the most important areas to shift and change if you really want to permanently alter your financial status. Like a thermostat in your home that maintains the temperature at the same level all the time, your self-image holds your current financial pattern in place. Even if your money programming is successful and you find yourself suddenly bringing in a lot of money, your self-image will eventually bring your income right back to where it was before, unless you consciously work to change it!

Your self-image is the image you hold of yourself. It consists of the following four things:

- How you "see" yourself
- How you talk to yourself
- What you think about yourself
- What your feel "comfortable" doing

In order to alter your income and overall relationship with money, you have to change all of the above views of yourself to that of a very wealthy person. If you can see, talk, think, and feel yourself as a wealthy

DAY 14

person, even just the smallest bit, you can begin to experience tangible changes in your income, in your earnings as well as savings. What if you were exactly like Bill Gates or Richard Branson? How would you think? How would you talk to yourself? What would you say to yourself when you wake up in the morning, throughout your day, and when you go to bed at night? What actions would you take and what things would you feel comfortable doing? Can you step out of your comfort zone? In fact, what is your comfort zone?

Changing your self-image means getting detailed and intimate with how you see, think, and do everything in your life because each of these things are part of the matrix that holds your wealth image together. Knowing and understanding your current image allows you to make different choices. If you recognize that you are cheap when it comes to spending money, you can find the beliefs and emotions that are at the base of those actions. If you find yourself saying "Oh, that's never going to happen," regarding taking a luxury vacation or purchasing a new car, then that is something you should explore and unravel.

How do you feel about walking down Rodeo Drive in Beverly Hills? How do you feel about hanging out at the Polo Lounge at the Beverly Hilton Hotel or even attending a polo match? As you imagine these things, notice how you feel. Does it frighten or intimidate you to be hanging out where the wealthy hang out? Does it make you angry "who wants to go there anyhow?" "Those people are so phony!" Or, do you love hanging out in such places, but secretly feel intimidated because you think the *wealthy* are better than you.

Visualization is a powerful tool that can augment the work you are doing and is not difficult to do. You can visualize your new life in the morning when you wake up or just before you fall sleep at night. Simply find a comfortable place to sit or lie down and when relaxed, close your eyes. Then, imagine that you are living in a wealthy neighborhood with wonderful neighbors, who are kind, caring, and loving people. In fact, they are all people just like you and may have started out with very little. Wealthy people aren't necessarily selfish, snobby or phony. If you think these things, realize they are YOUR beliefs and go directly to how you see, talk, think, and feel about yourself! Visualize that you are living in a mansion or an estate on the ocean or wherever the future, wealthy you is living. Walk through each room of the house. Touch the wood, smell the soap in the bathroom, touch the rich fabrics of clothing in your closet. Allow your imagination to explore and enjoy the new you who is living in this new life. A visualization does not have to be long or complex. Your goal is to lift your resonance by feeling the joy and happiness of living an abundant and prosperous life. When it feels complete, just open your eyes and go on with your day, or if at night, just drift off to sleep. Below are some steps to assist you to alter your image so that you can see yourself as the "new you."

STEPS TO THE NEW YOU:

1. Pick a model of who you'd like to be. Is there someone you know or know of that is very rich and whom you admire? Find someone who embodies all the qualities of the kind of person you want to be. Look for things you have in common with this person realizing that if they can do it, so can you!

2. See yourself differently. How do you currently see yourself? Look back on what you did the last few days. If this was a movie and you were watching yourself as a character in the movie, what traits would you notice? See yourself eating breakfast, having a cup of coffee with a friend, or even going shopping or for a walk. What do you notice about the way you walk? Talk? When you speak, what do you notice about the conversation and the things you say? Imagine that you step out of you own body and are watching yourself from across the room. What do you

DAY 14

notice about how this "you" talks, walks, speaks and gestures?

With this new perspective, give this "you" different traits. In this new scenario, see yourself taking on different traits and behaviors that a wealthy person would have, perhaps spending lavishly. See this new you in expensive clothes, driving a luxury car.

EXERCISE 13

FOUR STEPS TO CHANGING YOUR IMAGE

1. Create a picture of the goal you have written as your Statement of Desire. What will it look like when you have that $200 million dollars you want or when you are a billionaire. Imagine a snapshot has been taken of you holding the winning Lottery check, or in front of your newly purchased mansion, or sunbathing on your yacht. Write a description in your journal of this snapshot including descriptions of the items and the people in the photo. Include a detailed description of how much you have changed now that you are a multi-millionaire.

2. Think of someone you know or even have heard of who is extremely wealthy. What qualities does this person have?

3. Notice qualities that this wealthy person has. What qualities do you have that this very wealthy person also has? List those similar qualities in your notebook.

4. Imagine you have all the positive qualities you described above. Describe in your journal or notebook a day of your life that is the same as the life of the wealthy person you selected above. See yourself riding in your limousine, going shopping at Gucci's, or buying expensive jewelry at Winston Jewelers. Where do you go in your limo? Who do you meet? What kind of projects are you involved in?

5. How do you currently see yourself? If you watch yourself on a TV reality show, what traits do you notice? See yourself eating breakfast, having a cup of coffee with a friend, or even going shopping or for a walk. Write down the things you notice that you say, think, and do.

DAY 14

6. What new and different traits would you like to give to this "you" that you are seeing in this movie or TV reality show? Confidence? Esteem? Humor? Wisdom?

Write out what you discover in your notebook or journal.

DAY 14

I'LL SEE IT WHEN I BELIEVE IT

You are making great progress. You should be feeling inspired and excited about the potentials. You've set a money goal, whether that be $50,000 or $50,000,000. You've set a goal that should lift your resonance just because the possibility of it coming true is so incredibly exciting. All the exercises including the visualizations, meditations, and affirmations in this book are designed with the same goal in mind - to convince you to BELIEVE that your goal is not only possible, but that it WILL HAPPEN.

In this section, we are going to explore the little voice inside of you that says "It will never happen." This is the voice that you probably know is there, but have been afraid to address. Resonating in a high space is quite wonderful. It feels good to be in a space where an exceptionally prosperous future is a reality, but *what if...?* "What if I don't make it?" "What if it never happens?" The prospect that what you want will never happen carries a lot of weight and if it carries more weight than the belief that you CAN succeed, you know which part is going to win.

Your determination can also begin to wane as time passes and no tangible evidence shows up in your physical reality confirming that you are making progress toward your goal. Worse yet, is when things do start

DAY 14

showing up, but they scare you so much that you back away from the success. You already have lots of tools, including expanding your self-image, but it would really help a lot if that fear voice just went away altogether!

You've decided you want more money. You've also decided a number of other things that you know you don't want:

- *You don't want to struggle with money again*
- *You don't want to worry about having enough*
- *You don't want to be in debt*
- *You don't want to worry about whether you can afford something or not*

Your subconscious doesn't understand negatives. Saying "I don't want to worry" can be translated by the subconscious as "worry" or "I want to worry." You have to program the messages to the subconscious in a clear and specific way that effectively overrides old messages and beliefs, and you have to resolve the conflict that exists between wanting lots of money and the part of you that says "*No.*"

There are valid reasons why you developed fears that hold you back. The tendency to worry that you'll never be able to change and to feel sorry for yourself because "it just doesn't work for me" is a familiar pattern. To change image and identity to a whole new person, a person who never worries about money and who has unlimited wealth, can be a huge stretch into unfamiliar territory. It's scary.

The first thing to do is address the fear itself. What is the fear saying? Is it fear of failure? Is it fear of success because you might lose the "you" you know? What does that voice say? In the exercise below, you will be directed on how to talk and listen to this voice of fear and alter the conclusion you made, way back when, that "nothing works for me" and the fear that goes with it.

When you really want something, but are afraid to have it, a conflict occurs. The conflict is between the part of you that is determined to create a bountiful reality and the part of you that believes, based on past evidence, that it "just won't happen." Yes, you have evidence from your past of failures, but there is also evidence of success. Because it is inherent in each of us to do whatever is necessary to avoid pain, a lot of power is given to that fear voice. If you believe that what you want is going to cause pain, you're not going to want to go for it, are you?

Let's say, you decide you want to manifest a new car, but you already know you don't have enough money to buy it. How does that affect your thinking? In most instances, your attention diverts to what you don't have. "I don't have enough money to buy the car." It's not that you want to focus on the fact that you don't have enough money, but because you fear it, you find yourself thinking about it. Another example is you do a great job imagining you already have the car. You think about it and get excited about it, but as soon as you look at your checkbook, your logic kicks in and you find yourself saying "I don't have enough money." Your focus is redirected to thoughts and feelings of not having enough.

So, how do you break this vicious cycle? One of the best things you can do is focus on what makes you feel good. All of the visualizations and meditations in this book are designed to build your resonance to a high frequency of happiness, excitement, and enthusiasm and keep it going as long as possible. One way to do this is to focus on what makes you feel good and allow the emotions to take over.

Emotions are powerful generators, even more powerful than beliefs. When you focus on what makes you feel good, the emotional energy of those feelings builds and creates a magnetic frequency that attracts things in that same frequency. Does the idea of having great riches bring you pleasure? Does it make you feel good? By focusing on the good feelings, you are doing two things: you are resonating on the *feel-good* energy and you are not lying to yourself or creating internal conflict because all you

DAY 14

are doing is affirming that you FEEL GOOD. You can do this exercise when visualizing or meditating by just thinking about what you want. As we've been discussing, just think about what you want, visualize yourself in the situation, and self-talk about the feelings such imaging brings. Slowly and subtly, the idea imprints in your subconscious and emotionally, you can alter your feelings from one of "you can't have it" to one of "go get it."

In some instances, however, just feeling good and focusing on the positive, doesn't last. In fact, the natural high you experience from the happy resonance may be the very reason your fear starts escalating. If your subconscious has been programmed that "money is dangerous," for example, fear is going to be triggered. If you have a belief that "even when I win, I lose,", your subconscious is going to respond with a reality that starts showing loss. Perhaps its small at first, such as the utility bill goes up this month, or you get a notice that your insurance rates went up. They are all signs that perhaps you're hitting the glass ceiling, as the expression goes, and soon your subconscious belief that says, "don't go there" will kick in. In such an instance, putting on a happy face and ignoring the fear is dangerous!

There are lots of different techniques, but here is a fairly easy one that you can do by thinking it through and *listening*. The process involves giving voice to both parts, but seeking the highest intent or purpose of both. Start with the negative part tracing what it is seeking until you determine what is its highest goal. Then do the same with the second part until you discover that they both want the same thing. When you have reached a place where both conflicting parts are in agreement, close your eyes and imagine you are showing these two parts how much they agree. Imagine that as you bring your hands together, you are blending these two parts together, and they are now in agreement that they both want you to be "happy" or "loved" or "confident" or whatever the mutual quality is. Then imagine that you are pulling both of these energies into your heart, feeling them blend together. Thank them for assisting you and for providing for you all these years so you could reach this goal. When this exercise feels complete, write what you discovered in your notebook or in the exercises that follow.

EXERCISE 14

INTEGRATING PARTS

Follow this process and see what happens:

First step is to differentiate the two parts. Begin by focusing on the object of your desire, for example, increasing your annual income or getting a new, higher paying job. Get of sense of that energy and determine which hand represents that part.

Now, think about the opposite. What voice or feeling comes up that stops you from achieving this goal? Get a sense of the energy of this part and imagine that it is represented by the other hand. Describe what you discover:

Hold both hands out in front of you with palms up facing the ceiling. Select the hand that represents the part that is interfering with your goal of making and receiving great wealth. With eyes closed, imagine that this part is sitting on one of your palms. Think about what it does in your life and ask it what is its purpose in doing these things. What does it say? What does it do? For example, if it doesn't want you to have more money, ask what is its purpose in stopping you from having more money. Dialogue with it getting answers similar to the following:

> "Why do you stop money from coming into my life?"
> *"To keep you small."*
> "What is your purpose in keeping me small?"
> *"To keep you safe."*
> What is your purpose in keeping me safe?
> *"To keep you happy."*

Keep asking questions about its purpose until you feel you get to its highest purpose. Next, do the same thing with the positive part. First, identify what it does. Then ask what its purpose is in doing these things. As in the previous example, it might say:

> *"I get revved up and excited."*
> "What is your purpose in getting revved up and excited?"
> *"I get motivated."*
> "What is your purpose in getting motivated?"
> *"I start taking action."*
> "What is your highest purpose in taking action?"
> *"It makes me happy."*

Keep asking questions until you get to the highest purpose AND discover that its highest purpose is the same as that of the lesser part.

When you have reached a place where both conflicting parts are in agreement, that their purpose is the same, close your eyes again and this time imagine you are showing these two parts how much they agree. As you do this, slowly bring your hands together until they touch. When your hands touch, imagine these two parts are now blended and in agreement that they both want you to be "happy" or "loved" or "confident" or whatever the mutual quality is.

Still with eyes closed and hands blended together, pull both of these energies into your heart and feel them blend together into your heart. Thank them for providing all that they have provided all these years to reach that goal.

Write out what you discover in your notebook or journal.

DAY 15

STEPPING UP – THE ART OF MANIFESTING

Congratulations! You've reached a new pinnacle on your path toward great riches. Two weeks have passed since you started on this course. How are you doing? Have you been sticking with the program? Is your dedication to changing your money pattern still high? Is it waning?

You are half way through. Don't stop now! If you are considering stopping or you are beginning to slow down, now is a good time to evaluate why. If you stop at this point, what do you expect will happen? More than likely you are going to return to the way things have always been. As you saw in Chapter 12, old neural pathways are firmly imbedded and can only be overcome by continuous effort to reinforce new ones. You've been building the new pathways for only two weeks, while your old pattern has been operating since you were five or six years old! You've barely made a dent, but it is beginning.

If you joined a gym intending to lose 30 pounds and get your body tight and toned, would you quit after only two weeks? Of course not, and once you start to see evidence of changes, it gets more exciting and motivates you once more! In physical training, the first two weeks are just the warm up, getting your body used to the changes you are making, allowing the muscles to adjust to the intense attention they are now

DAY 15

receiving. But after the first two weeks, your muscles are ready to amp up! It's time for us to do that too!

Have you ever really wanted something and never let go of your resolve to get it? Do you remember how you did it? I remember one day when my dog ran away and I spent hours looking for him with no luck. As time passed and as day passed into night, I got more worried and frightened. I drove around the neighborhood calling his name, knocking on doors, asking neighbors if they'd seen a little white dog, but with no luck. Hours passed and I became more and more discouraged. I wanted to give up, but the outcome of losing my little dog was not acceptable. I refused to accept that I would not get my dog back. Even though thoughts of fear and doubt entered my mind, I stopped myself and refused to accept it. I just kept repeating, "*I'm getting my dog back.*" After more than nine hours, I went outside one last time and I saw him running down the sidewalk! Of course, I felt relieved, but I was also thrilled and overjoyed! I succeeded. I never gave up even when the odds seemed totally against me!

In manifesting anything, you must have this same level of commitment. Is there a similarity between manifesting more money and getting your dog back? I believe the similarity is the level of commitment. Think about any times when you held a level of commitment *no matter what!* I know of other times when I was waiting for an opportunity to come through. I may have been anxious, even fearful. I wavered. I'd hear myself saying, "This is never going to happen. Just let it go" and yet there was another part of me that stepped in and said, "No! I'm not letting this go." And, in the end I got what I wanted!

It doesn't matter if you waver; if you get discouraged. What matters is that you get back on track; that you remember the commitment and hold to it. A famous Chinese proverb says "*The man who says he never wins and the man who says he never loses are both right.*" You know this is true.

Whatever you put out there will repeat itself again and again. The same failure will occur in any endeavor, if you find yourself unable to hold your commitment or are unmotivated to reach for it.

You've been visualizing, meditating, and affirming new goals of great wealth and riches. The imagining you have been doing these past two weeks lifts your resonance to a high state because it is so exciting to anticipate and sense your financial dreams coming true. Your ability to dream is expanding and the muscle of your imagination is getting stronger and more adept at building a resonance of wealth. You may already be experiencing evidence of some shifts and changes such as finding coins or dollar bills, receiving an increase in your business income, or a surprise check arriving in the mail. If you were working out in a gym, your ability to do pushups would have probably expanded from doing two or three a day to ten or more. Physical trainers know that muscles can atrophy from lack of use and that it is important to continue to change the workout routines so your muscles are continually stretching and being challenged. Stretching and challenging yourself is just as important for your mind.

Manifesting is something you have been doing all of your life. Perhaps you remember when you were a child and you KNEW that Santa was going to bring exactly what you wanted or you KNEW you made the track team or that you got an "A" on your English test! For children, the limitations of a world of "no's" doesn't kick in as vigorously as many of us find in our later years. The key point here is that manifesting isn't an oddity or absurd exception to the rule. Manifesting is what we do, all the time, every day. Often, we only pay attention to upsetting or painful manifestations such as a past due tax bill, backed up traffic on the freeway, or an angry neighbor. But you are also manifesting the seven green lights you drove through on your way to work, the parking place right in front of the mall, and the extra check arriving in

DAY 15

the mail.

We are all born with an innate ability to have our thoughts materialize into physical form. This is something you already do and all we're talking about is becoming conscious of how you do it; giving yourself permission to manifest by choice and desire. The question isn't whether you have the power to manifest, but how to consciously take charge so you are manifesting what you want all the time!

Even though you know you are creating your reality all the time, most often you aren't conscious of what you are creating daily and how you are doing it. Most of us create by default. We're on auto-pilot acting more as an observer than a conscious creator of what is happening daily in our lives. When you do this, you are not paying attention to the frequency upon which you are operating every day. It's time to take charge of everything that is happening so that you are creating what you want all the time.

Become conscious of what you are thinking and feeling in the present moment. Set your intention of what you want and allow it to be what you choose! Below are the four primary steps to manifesting:

1. Know the details of what you want

The first secret to manifesting is to have a clear vision of exactly what you want. The more specific your intention, the easier it is to generate the energy you need to manifest it. Specific goals get specific results while wishy-washy goals get either no results at all or unclear wishy-washy ones.

Your desire also needs to be of something you truly want and which you can feel with intensity. Not a desire based on what you should do or need to do, but something you choose because you want it! A burning desire!

Your goal should also be something you really want, that stimulates you and makes you feel good every time you think about it. Do you speak about your goal with determination and conviction knowing that you will reach your goal no matter the obstacle? Do you really want it?

You've been resonating on the joy and excitement of being ultra-wealthy, but what is something very specific that you want to manifest now? It could be that you want to pay off a $5,000 credit card bill, or to pay off the loan on your car. Perhaps you have a business and you want to increase the number of clients or you just want to manifest a customer paying a $500 check. In thinking about what you want to manifest, select something you are passionate about. (And something you believe is possible.) If, for example, paying off your car brings a yawn or, just seems too big of a stretch, give this question more thought. What is something that excites you? Getting a raise? Getting one new account? A vacation? In the exercise that follows, there is a list of suggestions that may help you if you are having difficulty deciding on something that you want to manifest now. It is important that you find something that excites and inspires you because this is the energy with which you will be working.

2. **Build and hold the frequency**

Everything in the world has a frequency and when that frequency is combined with the frequency of *you*, a unique and powerful energy emerges. This is the energy that brings what you want into physical form. You can use tools you already have: your words, your desires, your thoughts, and your feelings to generate a frequency of what it feels like to have the thing you desire. The richer and deeper you allow yourself to feel these energies, the faster you will manifest what it is you want. On a scale from 1 to 10, select what you think is the level of the frequency you generate when you focus on the particular thing you want to manifest?

If your goal is a new car, for example, the brand, the style, the color, and even the smell of that new car, all combine to create a very specific energy that you are going to match in order to bring that specific thing into your life. On a scale of 1 to 10, what is the frequency of your desire

DAY 15

to have that car? Even receiving a check for $5000 or paying off a debt, has a specific energy to it. In order to manifest that specific thing, you are going to lift your resonance to match what it feels like to have the thing you desire, that very specific *thing*, because the energy for a new car is different than the energy of a $5000 check or even a new client. To build the resonance of what you want, start speaking to yourself out loud. What will this event or *thing* give you that you do not already have? Answer this question with great expression and detail. Here's an example:

> *Having this thing will give me great freedom. I will finally be able to live life the way I have always wanted to live. I will feel great joy and be able to share my joy with the people I love. It will allow me to feel and express my full potential. I will be so happy. I will feel empowered. It will affect how I feel everywhere I go whether that be traveling overseas or just shopping in the grocery store.*

If it helps, play inspirational music in the background as you express what having this person, event or thing in your life will give you. Stand and speak the words with great expression, feeling your energy and excitement building. On a gauge from 1 to 10, how high is your frequency of joy and excitement? If it is not yet to a level six or seven go back and evaluate what it is you are seeking? What's in the way of the joy and enthusiasm? Perhaps you have a fear or constricting belief that needs to be released. Perhaps there is something else you want even more. Work with it and with your energy, speaking your desire aloud, claiming what you want until you are at least at a level of 8 or 9! Practice building your resonance to a plus 10 frequency! Keep your focus and hold onto the excitement and the powerful feelings.

3. **Give thanks and let it go**

Sometimes, the desire to create or manifest something can come from anxiety or fear around NOT manifesting something you think you need. This is a resonance of anxiety or fear which will only serve to bring more of what you don't want. Remember, it is the resonance and energy that generates the frequency of what you desire. Your goal is to resonate on the frequency of the thing you want, combining that with the frequency of your desire and joy in accomplishing your goal. Once you can generate the frequency as close to a level 10 as possible, release the goal to the Universe allowing it to come back to you when the time is right. You don't let go of the desire, but rather release the time when it will manifest in your life, opening to receive it at the right place and right time. Say "Thank You" for all that you have and for what you are about to receive and then, let it go. It WILL come back!

4. <u>Act as if you already have it</u>

Now that you have released the "need" to have it now, continue with your day, continuing to be excited. It is just like it was when you were 6 or 7 and knew you were going to get that gift at Christmas or just like when you were in high school and knew that boy was going to ask you to the prom or when you knew you were going to get the job you wanted. You already know how to do this. It's about holding the resonance, knowing you are going to get what you want.

Imagine what it feels like that you can never fail. How does it feel to be unstoppable? This is the state where you are supposed to always be. You have already lifted your vibrational frequency by allowing yourself to get excited about being a multi-millionaire. Such a resonance level feels great and motivates you to stay there, right? Even if something happens that knocks you down, acknowledge what happened, forgive yourself for the slip up and get back into the high resonance as quickly as possible. With this knowledge, you can begin to create more and more of exactly what you want in your daily life. Practice. Perhaps you start with something small, *i.e.*, focusing on getting a parking place using

DAY 15

these same 4 steps:

1. Focus on what you want
2. Feel the energy of the "thing" you want, combining it with your desire to a level 10
3. Feel grateful and release it to the Universe
4. Follow through by taking action in your life that is in alignment with accomplishment of your goal

You know the expression: "If at first, you don't succeed, try, try again." Here is a perfect example of when to "try, try again." Your confidence will build as you begin to create more and more success and, more importantly, your resonance will automatically lift to a higher and higher level. This highly enlightened state of being becomes easier and easier to access when you are raising your vibration continuously. Remind yourself of this powerful truth:

I CAN HAVE ANYTHING I WANT!

Once you have reached the highest level you can reach on a scale from 1 to 10, close your eyes and imagine you are feeling gratitude for all you have, for all you will have, and for all the guidance and support you receive in your life. Imagine you are releasing this desire into the Universe, like releasing a helium balloon, watching it float off into the distance. As you watch it float away, feel the gratitude and joy of knowing that soon you will have this very thing in your reality.

Go on with the rest of your day or night continuing to resonate on the happiness, joy, and enthusiasm of the person, event or thing you are about to bring into your life. Leave the details of how it will manifest to the Universe which will bring it to you at exactly the right time and place. Continue to live your life knowing that this is already a part of your life and it is just a matter of time before the physical world catches up with the energy you have powerfully put in motion.

EXERCISE 15

MANIFESTING NOW!

Set Your Goal. What is something very specific that you want to manifest now? Select something you are passionate about. Find something that excites and inspires you. Write out a list of things that you want and then organize them into the highest priorities. Here's some ideas:

> a gift of money
> pay off a debt
> add a pool
> remodel your home
> take a vacation
> buy a vacation home
> refurnish your house
> buy a new car, boat, motorcycle, etc.,
> start a new career
> start a new business
> bring in a new high paying account
> win the lottery

2. Build a frequency of having what you want. Think about the thing or item you wrote in number 1 above. Imagine receiving or having this thing allowing yourself to feel how great it feels to have it. Build the resonance of what it feels like to have what you want. If necessary, play music to enhance the feelings. On a gauge from 1 to 10 - how high is your frequency of joy and excitement? If it is not yet to a level 6 or 7, go back and evaluate what it is you are seeking? What's in the way of that joy and enthusiasm? Perhaps you have a fear or constricting belief that needs to be released. Perhaps there is something else that you want even more. Work with it and with your energy, speaking your desire, claiming what you want until you are at least a level 8-9 on the scale. Speak out loud answering this question: What will this event or thing give you that you do not already have? Answer this question with great expression and detail, writing it out in your notebook or journal.

3. Thank and Release. Close your eyes. Feel gratitude for all that you have, for all that you will have and for all the guidance and support you receive in your life. Imagine you are releasing your desire into the Universe and watch it float off into the distance. Feel the gratitude and joy of knowing that soon you will have this very thing in your reality. Write in your journal how it feels to release and let this desire go, knowing it will be back to you soon.

4. Act as if. Go into your day or night resonating on the happiness, joy and enthusiasm of what you are about to bring into your life. Continue to feel the excitement of knowing that what you desire will soon manifest in your life. Write your thoughts and feelings about this in your notebook or journal.

DAY 16

DESERVING

On Day One, you were asked to make a written commitment to yourself, a commitment to change your financial future, and also a commitment that you will stick to this program for the next 30 days. In the big picture, 30 days is nothing when you think of all the years you have put into building and living a life of limitation. The exciting part, though, is that this book is showing more than just your limitations around money. As you discover limiting beliefs around earning, you can also see how these same beliefs have limited you in all aspects of your life from having nearly anything you want!

If you are sticking to the program, you've been discovering a lot of beliefs you hold about money, abundance, success and receiving and, now, we are going to talk about deserving or lack thereof.

Next to shame, lack of deserving is one of the most debilitating of all beliefs because it affects absolutely everything in your life. If you truly believe you don't deserve, the most powerful techniques in the world are not going to work. You will find yourself reaching out again and again, only to fall on your face most often with no idea of why. This subtle, often unspoken belief, is powerful and if ignored, will stop you from having

DAY 16

anything you want. Lack of deserving interferes with your efforts to manifest. It can fill you with guilt when you succeed. It can separate you from others and from your spirituality. It can freeze you in your tracks and open you to your own patterns of self-sabotage and self-punishment. No matter how hard you fight for success, if you don't believe you deserve to have it, you will watch your success slowly fall apart or even worse find yourself flat on your back wondering what in the heck just happened.

Lack of deserving isn't something that is easy to spot. Unless you find yourself saying the words, "I don't deserve," you may think a recent failure is simply lack of confidence, self-sabotage, or even self-punishment. Perhaps you have worked with these different emotions and energies, rebuilding your confidence and then the same disastrous results occur. If you believe you don't deserve, it is going to show itself. So, it is very important to address it now.

Merriam-Webster dictionary defines the word *deserve* as follows:

have or show qualities worthy of reward or punishment; merit, earn, warrant, rate, justify, be worthy of, be entitled to, have a right to, be qualified for, justified, justifiable; due, right, just, fair, fitting, appropriate, suitable, proper, apt;

There are a lot of overlaps in this definition to issues of self-worth and self-esteem, but also notice the connection to *earning*. We previously defined earning as the effort you put into obtaining what you want, but it also includes how successful you have been in actually getting what you want. As a child, you were taught that the best route to feeling deserving was to win the approval of others. This may have included working hard, being kind, being honest, turning the other cheek, perhaps suffering or sacrificing for the good of others, and even withdrawing into the shadows to let someone else gain the spotlight. The problem with such lessons is that they not only contradict many of your goals of *having what you want*, but with such beliefs, you will never give yourself permission to shine. If you are seeking approval of others, you will always fail on some level because there will nearly always be someone who will disapprove. Your best will never be enough and no matter how good a job you do, you will still feel you failed in some way. As shown in the above definition, you only deserve if you "do something or have or show qualities worthy of reward or punishment."

As a teenager, or even in your early twenties, you were probably unstoppable. You no doubt truly believed you could do anything, and often, it isn't until mid-life that you realize your life never quite went as you had expected. Broken relationships, lost dreams, and failed opportunities take their toll. You now look back evaluating whether you have "done something" or "have or show qualities worthy of reward or punishment." You form judgments about yourself based on messages you received years prior and conclusions you made long ago. The conclusions you make now are no longer based on seeking approval of others, but on failed approval of yourself. Lack of deserving permeates your thoughts and feelings; affects your choices and infiltrates your beliefs. Even if you've never seriously evaluated past mistakes and failures, there are usually judgments hiding there. Now, you are working hard to be wealthy beyond anything you have ever experienced before. Do you deserve it? "I've failed so many times! I don't deserve to succeed now!" Such conclusions push your desires out of reach. What you seek and long for is unavailable. You believe "you can't get there from here."

You are learning new techniques and processes to release restrictive beliefs and patterns. You are learning to build your resonance to one of financial bounty and success, and as you do so, you may be feeling a combination of two strong feelings: *excitement and fear*. No doubt you are excited about the new potentials, but with success there is always fear - fear that you might fail; fear that you won't be able to maintain the

DAY 16

success. There may even be a part of you that knows you will fail because that part knows you hold a belief that you don't deserve to win, to have bounty and abundance, or to be happy. Whatever those beliefs may be, they need to be released so you can continue on your way towards great wealth! Before you proceed further, you need to alter limiting beliefs you may have about deserving so you can create the abundance you desire.

Whether you truly believe you deserve to have great wealth or not, isn't really the issue because any such belief is not rooted in truth. Though ministers and priests of different faiths may speak of the importance of deserving, there is no truth to it. The concept was taught to you by people, and perhaps a culture, who were more concerned about what other people think than who you truly are or what you really want. If you continue to let *other people's* standards direct your life, you will never accumulate great wealth. Remember 98% of the world is NOT wealthy! Are you really concerned about getting their approval? Is such a thing even possible? Obviously, not! It is time for you to evaluate your own determination of what is right, what has merit, what is *suitable for reward* and whether you want to continue to follow such standards. You need to make that decision consciously. You are already making value judgments about yourself, but are they really helping you? Let's take a deeper look and make some internal changes so you can create the financial windfall you desire.

Now is the opportunity to look at what you learned about deserving and how you are playing it out in your current life. Review your past and what you learned from your parents, your teachers, and society itself. What unresolved emotions resulted in judgments about what you deserve? What secrets do you have from your past that you've never addressed that may stop you from really creating great success now? What shames do you still carry that pop up when you get close to success?

And, how do you play it out? Do you feel guilty when you succeed? Ashamed? Do you hold yourself back and never act? Do you take things away to punish yourself for past misdeeds? To have the great success you can truly have, you must give yourself full permission to create over-the-top success and to reap the bounty of such success. To do that, you need to forgive yourself for past shames, failings, and mistakes. You need to evaluate where you may stop yourself because of judgments that "you don't deserve that!" In other words, you need to really love yourself and give yourself permission to fulfill your dreams now! Don't pass up this opportunity to heal this subtle but debilitating belief.

In the exercises that follow, you have an opportunity to uncover the beliefs that may be holding you back along with steps to overcome them and get back on track to creating your greatest success – more wealth than you ever imagined possible.

EXERCISE 16
DESERVING

Write answers to the following questions.

1. What messages do you recall receiving as a child about deserving? Look for messages from parents or caregivers where you were told things like: "You don't deserve to have nice things." "What makes you think you deserve to have something for nothing?" "People who aren't nice, don't deserve to be rich!" Or, "Because you worked so hard, you deserve a special treat."

2. What do you recall about when you first felt undeserving. Where did it start? How did it start?

3. Evaluate your relationship with mother and then with father. How do you think those relationships affected your decision about what you deserve? Were there any angers or hurts that you failed to address as a child that you may have converted into a decision that you don't deserve?

4. What is your pattern of undeserving? What does it do to you? For example, if you feel you don't deserve something, do you feel guilty? Ashamed? Do you punish yourself? Do you numb out your feelings? Freeze in your tracks? Does it cause illness?

5. If someone else is successful in obtaining what you've been seeking, how do you feel about it? Resentful? Angry? Depressed?

6. How do you hold yourself back from having what you want? For example, do you prevent yourself from doing or having something because you feel guilty? Wrong? Scared that you will be judged? Do you

numb out?

7. In what ways do you find yourself unable to take action on something you want? How does it make you feel? Numb? Sorry for yourself? Resentful? Powerless?

8. How do you feel about failures from your past? Does succeeding now cause you to judge those failures, *i.e.*, "I don't deserve to be wealthy after all those times in my past when I failed." What judgments have you formed about yourself and your past?

9. What are the pay-offs, the benefits of not being deserving? For example, do you get to feel sorry for yourself? Do you get to avoid responsibility? Do you get to stay where you're at and not move forward?

10. Do you feel you are deserving of good things, or do you feel you have to do something to earn them? Write out your thoughts and feelings about how you deserve or don't deserve.

Use the techniques that you have learned in prior chapters to assist you to change beliefs that you don't deserve. And, if all else fails move forward in this book to the chapter on forgiveness.

DAY 17

POWER OF THE FUTURE

The future is a powerful and often intimidating concept. We all want to believe that the future will be great and hope it will be even better than anything we have experienced in the past, but often people are afraid of the future. Often, they just don't want to look. But what if there is an entirely new paradigm that is completely different than anything you have been told or imagined? What if that new paradigm is no longer one where the past creates the present, but one where the future does. The very idea may be mindboggling at first, but bear with me for a few moments while I explain. There is a reason this is important when it comes to creating more abundance and prosperity in your life.

Quantum physicists have discovered that the future is a powerful force. It not only may influence the present, but theories are spinning in the quantum physics world that the future, not the past, is creating the present. This means that your relationship with the future is more important than ever with regard to manifesting and creating what you want in your life. Noted physicist, Fred Alan Wolf, has said:

DAY 17

> *There is a real mathematical basis for saying actions in the future can have an effect on the probability patterns that exist in the present. In other words, what takes place now, what choices are being made right now, may not be as free to you as you think they are.*[6]

Even if you understand this possibility, taking it in at a deep level and operating from this knowledge can be a completely different thing. Life can get difficult when things aren't going the way you planned; when hopes and dreams get dashed and when, after years and years of working so diligently on yourself, you find yourself still experiencing a less than magnificent life. This is not, however, evidence of an old paradigm at work, but is simply evidence that your present is being influenced - even created, by a negative future. If the future you are headed toward is filled with pain and struggle, you aren't going to want to see it. You won't even want to think about it or even look. Who would?

But if the future is influencing, even creating the present, then it also holds immense power. We know that no one is a prisoner of the past, but it is easy to project painful memories and expectations into the future based on that past. We also know that wherever you put your focus and intention, will magnify and grow. Thus, focusing on problems of the past magnifies them, but projecting into the future all that you want, visualizing what you want that future to be, supports and augments all the work you have already been doing in this program. Thus, it is more important than ever to know where you are headed and to change that path if it is anything less than magnificent!

Imagine that in the future, you are living an amazing life, where you have accomplished every dream and every goal with aplomb. As you think, imagine, and start dreaming about this positive future, you immediately feel different. Such imagining alters who you are in the

---

[6] Interview with Fred Alan Wolf, www.intuition.org/txt/wolf.htm

present. It lifts your spirits and puts a smile on your face. This is the power of the future at work and because the future can be whatever you choose it to be, you have the power to make it as magnificent as you desire. Your dreams and visions all reside in the future. Focusing on the accomplishment of your dreams in the future has an energy and a realness that is grander and more powerful than just visualizing possibilities. As quantum physicists are discovering,

> *a belief reflects ... a message from a future waiting to be realized. In quantum physics, we deal with possible futures all of the time. They are possibilities as seen from a perspective of the present moment. But realities as seen from the time the event occurs in the future. In other words, in parallel universes all events occur across the landscape of time.*[7]

Your dreams and visions can be both a point of focus and a means of connecting to the future you desire. For over two weeks, you have been resonating in a new place and on a new frequency that everyone agrees feels pretty darn amazing. This frequency is a result of your focus and attention on what is possible - dreaming it, imagining it, and ultimately expecting it. The power of the future can be a powerful ally to building that expectation!

By holding attention on a positive future, the future can aid you in your journey forward because it will pull you to it. It aids in reaching your dreams because it continues to call you to it. All you need to do is remember and hold your attention on it. You do that by dreaming! Imagining! Visioning!

As part of your progress toward manifesting great wealth, you are developing and enhancing multiple tools, from affirmations to visualizations, from changing beliefs to reprogramming your

---

[7] www.intuition.org/txt/wolf.htm; **Fred Wolf**

DAY 17

subconscious. And now you can add paying attention to the future, choosing and designing exactly where you are headed, resonating on futures that hold the energies of the wealth and abundance you have always wanted. You have dreams that you may have lost over the years; visions of what the world can be and what your life can be. You are envisioning living in a multi-million-dollar house, driving a Rolls-Royce, and being a multi-millionaire. It's time to reaffirm the dreams and expand the vision. Your dreams and visions of what can be are your direct connection to a positive future.

Keep dreaming. Expand your visions of what is possible. Connections to positive futures are magnetic and will pull you forward. Let the future be the powerful ally that it can be and use it to keep you focused on where you are going and what you want it to be!

Dream and vision boards aren't new. People have been creating dream boards for years by posting images from magazines onto poster board as reminders of what is possible. A vision board is a collage of images and pictures of things you want in your life. Get clear about your goals by finding images of things you want to manifest. Search online for photos, quotes, stories that can stimulate your excitement and enthusiasm about the future you are putting in place where all your dreams are fulfilled.

Use the vision board to focus your mind on what you want to create. As always, the goal is to keep your resonance high in anticipation of all you are going to create in your future. There is a story that Oprah created a vision board for Obama before he was elected. In the center, she put a photo of Obama and next to him she put a photo of the dress she was going to wear to his inauguration. All the things she put on her vision board came to pass!

Creating your personal vision board can help you imagine all that you want to create in your future. Put it some place where you will see it regularly as a reminder of all your dreams and goals and to keep yourself excited about what is going to be!

EXERCISE 17
YOUR VISION FOR THE FUTURE

1. Create a Wish List

Write 10 things in your notebook that you would like to be, to do, or have. Give your list a title and date. Put the list some place where you will see it regularly reviewing it often. This list of what you want in your future will ultimately affect the small decisions you make every minute of every day. Though you remember the big decisions, such as getting married, taking a new job, moving to a new house, it is the little decisions that ultimately lead you to fulfillment of your wishes.

2. Create a Vision Board:

After doing your wish list, start looking for images of things on your list. Prepare your vision board by cutting out images and pasting them on the board. Write some affirmations that support your future goals.

3. Write a Future Script

Using your vision board and referring to your Wish List, write a story (in present tense) of what your life is like in this future where you have all of the things on your list and board. Write it as though it is happening now.

DAY 18

MOTIVATION

How good are you at sticking with your goals? How well have you been doing following through on the suggestions and exercises in this book? After two and half weeks, we are going to stop and check your progress.

For over two weeks you have been guided to lift your resonance to one of abundance, prosperity, and success. Two days ago, you raised your resonance even more by focusing on a smaller goal and building your excitement and enthusiasm around why you want it.

On the first day of this program, you made a commitment to yourself to alter your financial reality. You prepared a Statement of Desire and promised to read it aloud twice a day. Each time you repeat the words on your Statement of Desire, you are reaffirming the commitment you made on Day One. If you stopped affirming this desire after a few days or after only a week or two, you are confirming with your subconscious that you don't really want to change. You are confirming a pattern of starting things that you don't finish. As you know, longing to have more without taking steps to bring about change, just holds the old pattern in place. Your subconscious knows this pattern well and accepts the

DAY 18

message that things are supposed to remain the same. "*I'll never get what I want*" has been around far longer than your desire to be a "*multi-millionaire by the end of the year.*" The neural pathways that hold your limited money pattern in place remain intact. Remember that to change them, you need to repeat the new pattern at least 30 times!

So, at this midway point, let's evaluate your level of commitment. If it is low or lacking, there is no point in continuing. Going through the motions each day with no effort and no intention of succeeding is no different than putting a book next to your bed that you never read. Good intentions do nothing when it comes to manifesting your goals and dreams.

You can talk yourself into quitting anything, but there is also a part of you that believes it is possible to change your financial future. If not, you wouldn't have started this book. Let's focus on these two *parts*. These are probably the same two parts you discovered on Day 13, the one that wants to change your financial future and the one that doesn't think it will ever happen. Which one will win and why?

Resonance is a powerful magic. No matter what your goal may be, the more you resonate on the emotions that support what you desire, such as joy, happiness, excitement, and enthusiasm, the sooner the object of your desire will manifest. There is a catch, however, as you raise the level of desire and commitment, resistance will also be triggered. If you are resonating on the joy and passion you feel knowing you will have your dream car, your belief that such cars are dangerous or that having what you want brings loss will also be triggered. Does this mean you should stop? Does this mean you should quit? Of course not! Perhaps the ordinary guy or gal out there may crumble under the pressure, but you have a great deal of knowledge and many tools. You now have a great tool for changing beliefs. You can stretch your image! You can alter programs in your subconscious. Why would you choose to go back to the life of the Lesser, when you have all the tools you need to be the More!!

In order to truly change your reality to one of abundance, you need to stick to the program: *Lift your resonance and keep it high. If you fall, pick yourself up and keep going.* Find the winner in you that crosses the finish line even if you don't come in first place! Napoleon Hill, author of the famous book, "Think and Grow Rich," coined the phrase "*Winners never quit and quitters never win.*" Which are you?

Now is a good time to evaluate where you are at, not only in this program, but in your life. Unless you can answer this question with "*My life is amazing*" or "*I'm getting everything I want*" then you are not doing what you need to do to lift out of a "*less than*" reality. You were forewarned that this program would take work. This is because the old patterns are firmly set and have been honed daily for decades. Those neural pathways were set in place many years ago and will only change through intention, consistency, and repetition.

There are two *parts* in you that we met a few days back: one that wants to win and another who says, "I can't do it." These *parts* have a lot of power and are each determined to hold onto the power they have. If you continue to feed them, they will remain strong and keep their hold on you. So, it is important to not only recognize these inner *voices,* but to feed the positive ones and stop feeding the negative ones. How do you feed them? By giving them your attention through your thoughts and inner dialogue. Just as you now know that unused neural pathways will shrivel and disappear through lack of use, so will these negative parts if you refrain from giving them your attention.

You have two options in dealing with these negative parts: (1) feed the part that wants to be rich and wealthy with continuous reminders, affirmations, visualizations, meditations, photos, and quotes, or (2) you can feed the other part with the exact same techniques! It isn't the technique that changes your resonance, but what you put into it! The

DAY 18

negative part is going to knock you down. It is going to repeat the *"same 'ol, same 'ol."* It uses the exact same techniques as the positive voice: thoughts, feelings, affirmations *i.e.,* "Nothing works for me" "Why bother?" "I'm a loser." "Nothing I do ever works" and other reminders and non-stop negative talk. Negative thinking even alters your posture, your facial expression, the way you walk and talk. If someone were to take a snapshot of you when you are not looking, what kind of look would you have on your face?

It's interesting in this day of *reality television* that we watch TV shows of people living their lives and see all the mistakes and craziness in their lives. What would you see if you watched yourself? Who is that person you are playing every day of your life and who is the person you are becoming through the positive affirmations and techniques you are learning in this book? As you check your progress, what do you discover? Do you see yourself developing the More of you and continuing forward no matter what? Or, do you see your Lesser stepping in, objecting and balking at the changes you are making and slowly taking over, only to allow you to return to the way you have always been, struggling for money or just making enough?

There is only one way to win and that is to be a winner all the time. It's easy to be strong and at ease when things are going well. The true test is when things get tough; when the challenges set in. That's when you need your strength and wisdom more than ever. Evaluate where you are at in this program. How strong is your commitment? If you started out strong and now are getting lazy or are beginning to feel sorry for yourself, ask yourself why would you do that? Why would you allow that? It's only been two weeks!

Yes, resistances will show up, but you have powerful tools that work. If you find you are getting scared, then work with the fear. Write it out. Give it a mode of expression, writing and writing and writing. Change the belief that's holding it in place and pull yourself back into a positive frame of mind.

Get excited and motivated. If you aren't excited about your goal, then change the goal. Pick one that does inspire and excite you. If things are happening in your reality counter to what you've been programming, figure out what it means. Your reality is an expression of your inner thoughts and feelings. It is a metaphor. If there is a conflict between what you want and what you are getting, do the Integrating Parts technique in Chapter 14. Maybe you need to do some forgiveness work. Maybe you need to do some inner child work. If self-pity is your drug of choice, learn every single aspect of it so you can forever walk away and never allow it to affect you again. These are all choices that are empowered choices. Remember the words of Napoleon Hill "Winners never quit and quitters never win!"

When resistances show up, realize they are only showing up because the work you are doing is changing things. If not, there would be no reason to resist. When resistances show up, don't back away from your progress. Instead, step up with more force and positive intention than ever before. If someone is in a terrible relationship and never objects, the controlling partner will probably relax and be comfortable because the *status quo* is remaining intact, but, if one partner starts to show evidence they are going to leave, do you think the controlling partner will remain relaxed? Do you think they will ignore the changes, smile and look the other way? Of course not! They are going to amp up their objections and fight to hold onto that person and to the relationship.

If you are experiencing resistance to change, now is the time to take stock of what the resistance is and how it shows itself. What's your inner bully and how does it work? What tools does this inner bully use to get you to back down and go back to the status quo? Fear? Anger? Self-pity?

Self-pity can take a lot of different forms. It can show up as feeling sad

DAY 18

and sorry for yourself, but it can also show up as anger, confusion, and despair. Anything that makes you feel sorry for yourself has self-pity behind it. "My car battery went out." "My computer won't work." "I don't have enough money." "I lost my wallet!" What do you say because of the problems that seem to catch your attention over and over?

You know these are resistances, but how do you respond? What's your pattern? If you still find yourself struggling, angry, and resentful because your processing isn't working, how are you going to find a way out? Yes, there's a voice in there that confirms your negative voices are right! Your life really is more difficult than anyone elses'. You really do have computer problems that no one else ever has. You really do work harder than anyone else and "nothing works for you." Your subconscious will support ANY BELIEF YOU PUT IN IT!

You started this program two and a half weeks ago, so if resistances are just coming up now, that's not bad. Will the resistances increase? Sure, they will if you ignore them, but you have tools that the average person does not have! You now have a powerful changing technique that you learned in Chapter 8 that works to change beliefs! You know how to integrate conflicting parts; you know how to talk to your subconscious. You have tools that are designed to assist you. Use them to move beyond any resistances that may be stopping you from reaching your goal.

Wealthy people aren't lucky people. They have losses and disappointments just like everyone else. They have spouses who betray them, kids who overdose, businesses that fail, tax bills, law suits, and foreclosures, but they keep going anyhow. A truly successful person, will pick themselves up again and again and still cross the finish line. So what if they came in third or 50th! They kept going and you can too. It is a choice. You may now be saying that none of the above applies to you. You've been reading each chapter in this book and doing *some* of the exercises. "I didn't do the one yesterday or three days ago, but I have other priorities that take up my time." To that I have to ask the question: why isn't creating great wealth and abundance your number one priority?

Check your motivation today. Just like a race car driver who after a few turns around the track, pulls off to the side for a pit stop. They check the tires. They add oil to the engine. They tighten any lose bolts or cables and then get back into the race. This is *pit stop time*. Stop and evaluate where you are in this 30-day program. How are you doing? Check your motivation. Where is it at today compared to last week or to two weeks ago, when you first started?

Are you as excited as you were on Day One? Are you as motivated as you were 18 days ago? If so, great! Keep going! Get pumped up. But, if not, then find out why and change it! This is YOUR future we're talking about and you have the power and ability to make it what you want it to be.

Listen to inspirational recordings today to lift your spirits and remind yourself that the MORE of you does know how to do this; that there is Greatness in You and that this part can carry you through to victory. Go online and type in the words "inspirational recordings" in any search engine. You will find hundreds of them. Listen to as many recordings you need to listen to until you feel motivated again. Remember, anything is possible. Even if you get discouraged, that will pass and you can get back on track. Though this book is designed with lessons over a period of 30 days, no one is evaluating you other than yourself. You can repeat the same chapter and the same exercises over and over again as many times as you like. Do whatever you need to do to accomplish your long-term goals. You can take your time and finish the book and exercises in 60 days. In fact, a recent study showed that contrary to popular belief,

DAY 18

the average person takes 66 days to change a habit![8] You know yourself better than anyone and know your process and what it takes for you to accomplish your goals. Trust that about yourself. Just don't give up! You can do this!

At the end of this chapter you will find some great quotes from some very powerful, successful people. Each one shows core beliefs they each hold that have propelled them to success. If you have limiting beliefs that stop you or that even may be slowing you down, why in the world would you keep them? Why in the world would you continue to operate on such beliefs when you have the POWER to create and operate on completely different ones? You can totally alter your life to one of great success and achievement, but you need to hold the same powerful, core beliefs as each of the successful people quoted below. Read each one and see if you operate on any of these same beliefs.

> *I want to be the person that is the first person there and the last person to leave. That's who I want to be, because I think the road to success is through commitment, and through the strength to drive through that commitment when it gets hard. And it is going to get hard and you're going to want to quit sometimes, but it'll be colored by who you are, and more by who you want to be.* — Will Smith

> *Champions are not the ones who always win races - champions are the ones who get out there and try. And try harder the next time. And even harder the next time. 'Champion' is a state of mind. They are devoted. They compete to best themselves as much, if not more, than they compete to best others."* --- Simon Sinek

> *I've failed over and over and over again in my life and that is why I succeed."* --- Michael Jordan

---

[8] Philippa Lally, health researcher for University College London; published in the European Journal of Social Psychology, July 2009

When you get into a tight place and everything goes against you, till it seems as though you could not hang on a minute longer, never give up then, for that is just the place and time that the tide will turn. --
- Harriet Beecher Stowe

I don't care how good you are, how talented you are, how much you work on yourself. There are times when things just won't go right. When anything that can happen will happen. You must have faith. You've gotta believe in yourself, believe in your abilities, your service, your company, your ideas. You've gotta have faith cause faith will give you patience. --- Unknown

"Even if you get knocked down, you get back up. You get back up and you continue to get back up!" --- Unknown

The secret of your success is determined by your daily agenda.
— John C. Maxwell

There's no maybe. You've gotta get up and say I'm going to be a champion. You need to do whatever it takes.
--- Arnold Schwarzenegger

Take up one idea. Make that one idea your life - think of it, dream of it, live on that idea. Let the brain, muscles, nerves, every part of your body, be full of that idea, and just leave every other idea alone. This is the way to success. --- Swami Vivekananda

You may encounter many defeats, but you must not be defeated. In fact, it may be necessary to encounter the defeats, so you can know who you are, what you can rise from, how you can still come of it.
— Maya Angelou

It does not matter how slowly you go as long as you do not stop.
--Confucius

Trust yourself. Create the kind of self that you will be happy to live with all your life. Make the most of yourself by fanning the tiny, inner sparks of possibility into flames of achievement.
— Golda Meir

DAY 18

Success is not final; failure is not fatal: it is the courage to continue that counts. — Winston Churchill

A passionate belief in your business and personal objectives can make all the difference between success and failure. If you aren't proud of what you're doing, why should anybody else be?
— Richard Branson

Desire is the key to motivation, but it's determination and commitment to an unrelenting pursuit of your goal - a commitment to excellence - that will enable you to attain the success you seek.
— Mario Andretti

"Anyone who lives within their means suffers from a lack of imagination."
– Oscar Wilde

"Never, never, never give in!" — Winston Churchill

EXERCISE 18
MOTIVATION

1. Write a full paragraph of all the reasons why you don't want to finish this book.

2. Next, write out at least one full paragraph on why you want to complete this book and all the exercises and what you expect to obtain if you do.

3. Imagine that you are at your 100th birthday and people are praising you for your accomplishments throughout your life. Write out the speech that one or more of the guests will read at your party.

4. Write a short paragraph on something that impassions you such as righting injustices, helping people overcome adversity, art, music or dance. If you can't think of anything, then just start with this sentence: *"Something that makes my heart sing is …"* then just trust whatever flows from your mind to your pen or keyboard. You may be delighted at what comes out.

DAY 19
AVENUE OF MANIFESTATION

Since the start of this book, we've been focusing on dreams - dreams about money, dreams about great wealth, and all the things it can buy. For some, it's a stretch to go from deep debt or having barely enough to imagining great wealth. All that means, however, is you need to work a bit harder to stretch your self-image and perhaps work a little longer before you will see a manifestation of wealth. Everything in this universe holds a frequency of energy. You are changing your money frequency to allow more and more wealth into your life. Today, we are going to discuss creating an avenue for the flow of that wealth.

Your resonance lifts your energy and raises your personal wealth vibration or frequency, however, if you do not have a viable avenue for the flow of that wealth, it is going to be difficult to see evidence of changes in your finances. It's like a dam that holds back water. The water will seep wherever there is a weak spot. Dams are designed to hold and reserve water, but a dam must have some way of releasing water in a controlled way, an outlet valve of some type. You also need such an outlet, an avenue of least resistance through which money can flow to you easily and effortlessly.

DAY 19

No doubt, you already have a flow of money into your life through a job, a business, perhaps from a pension fund or a social security check. Your current means of receiving money is the most believable place for money to arrive because you have already been living a reality where money comes from that source. Now, however, you are expanding your money image and resonating on a higher level of income. As money comes in, it still has to fit in with your logic and reason. If it doesn't, you won't accept it. You won't receive it. For example, if someone was to ring your doorbell and hand you a briefcase full of a thousand $1000 bills, you would probably back away and refuse to accept it. You accept the idea that anything is possible as an intellectual concept, but a briefcase full of a thousand $1000 bills seems suspicious. If, however, Publisher's Clearing House showed up at your door with balloons and a check for $1,000,000, it might still frighten you, but you would accept it because you believe it is possible to *win* a million dollars.

The question that exists with manifesting great wealth in your current reality is whether your current source of income can logically provide you with millions of dollars. Do you believe it is possible? If, for example, you are currently working at McDonalds for $10 an hour, is it realistic that your first million will flow from that job? Probably not. Perhaps you can stretch the possibility by imagining that you become an owner of the McDonald's restaurant, but then there is another question to ask. Is owning a fast food restaurant what you want? If so, great, but if not, then what is it that you do want that can provide you with great joy as well as great wealth? To be creating millions doing work that you love is the greatest and most rewarding avenue for manifesting wealth. Right now, you may already be seeing signs that your new resonance is working, but to increase your wealth to that of a millionaire, it is important to also expand your dreams so you can allow the avenue through which that wealth will arrive to be a part of your new resonance.

MONEY MAGICALLY

This doesn't mean you stop anything you are currently doing. You want to continue to focus on great wealth and the *things* that you want from that great wealth. You already know that big money resonance is different than small money (or no money) resonance and are doing a number of different things to lift your resonance, including reading your Statement of Desire twice daily, repeating affirmations, visualizations, and meditations. The whole key is to keep your focus on what you want AND to feel what it feels like to already have what it is you want. Today, we are expanding this work by including an avenue through which these great riches can flow.

Wealthy people have multiple sources of income. So, it is not about finding just one thing that will produce great income, but finding one thing NOW that will produce greater income than you are currently receiving. If you already have a job with great potential or a business you enjoy or a good pension plan, any of these can be the basis of expanding your image along with your income. If you do not currently have any of these things, however, then it's time to design and focus on this new expansion. In a sense, you are building your dream of great wealth on top of your dream of the work you truly want to do in the world. Let's get more specific and detailed about what that is. In this way, you are making the option of great wealth a more real possibility. It is more believable that you can manifest great wealth if you have a realistic, plausible means for generating that wealth. And, if you see this wealth coming through something you truly love to do, it's going to accelerate exponentially! The goal is to expand your imagination to include another dream that will be the basis for your great wealth.

Here's some suggestions on how to create and expand your avenue of manifestation:

- **Decide what you want**. This point may involve designing and creating a whole new business or focusing in more detail on

DAY 19

something you already have. The number one rule to manifesting is to focus in detail on what it is you want. If you are not sure of what that is, take the time to figure it out. Put your dreaming to use. Allow your imagination to open and start dreaming of what your life will be like when you have great wealth along with the source of that wealth. What is your passion? In what ways can you turn your passion into something that creates incredible riches? Is it a business? Is it a charity? Is it a career that pays big wages with amazing opportunities and contacts? Is it an expansion of your current business with more visibility and a larger clientele? Perhaps it is something entirely new and different from anything you ever thought possible. Detail your dream.

- **Imagine the details**. Expand your imagination. How can this business, job, or opportunity make you wealthy? This is where you start painting in the details. See yourself at your place of work. Perhaps you are a real estate investor and you have a beautiful office inside your home. Or, it could be a job where you are traveling worldwide working with famous people, meeting political figures or icons of industry. Perhaps your income arrives from a successfully published book. Expand. Dream big, big, big.

- **Feel the success**. Allow yourself to feel what it feels like to have incredible success. Imagine you are already doing these things and feel all the emotions that go with it. What is this business or opportunity giving you that you don't already have? If it is increased clientele or more visibility in your work, feel it as though it is happening now. As you did on Day 14, feel the excitement and raise it to a level 10 or as close as possible. Let the details expand as you watch the movie of this successful venture, feeling how it feels to be doing work you love and receiving great wealth in the process. Feel it with intensity. Hold it in your thoughts with passion and allow enough time for it to manifest.

The happiest, most successful people on the planet are all doing something they love, creating something they believe in, living a life of purpose and passion. Do the exercises in the next section to add the dream of doing what you love as the avenue for bringing in great wealth.

EXERCISE 19

CREATE AN AVENUE FOR MANIFESTING YOUR FORTUNE

Write answers to the following questions & exercises:

1. Make a list of 20 things you really enjoy doing in your life, even if you haven't done some of them in a long time. Then answer each of the additional questions in the chart below. Suggestions may be things like: "walking on the beach, traveling, playing volleyball, listening to music; dancing, reading, talking with friends, singing...."

20 Things You Enjoy	Alone or with others?	Costs money or free?	Involves people or things?	Risky or Non-risky?	Last time you did this?

MONEY MAGICALLY

2. What kind of business or opportunity can you create using as many of the things on the above list as possible? Write down all ideas that come up no matter how farfetched they may seem. For example, if you have the following on your list of things you love: "traveling, working with people, being creative, party planning, listening to music" a possible opportunity might be putting together incentive travel for big companies such as award banquets or business conferences. Another example may be: "working from home, movies, writing, learning new things" and the end result might be an independent blog writer, a script writer, etc.

3. Use the power of the future to see your ideal future career or money creating venue. Imagine you are 5 years into the future. Meet with your Future Self and have them show you their life in the future. Where do you live? What businesses or opportunities are you doing in that future that is producing great wealth? Write out in detail all that you see and experience in that future.

4. Expand the experiences you saw in that future to become an over-the-top success. If you are a healer, for example, see yourself as world famous, healing people all across the planet. If you are an artist, see yourself selling your art worldwide for hundreds of thousands of dollars, being interviewed on television, etc. If you own a company, see yourself

EXERCISE 19

running it with hundreds of employees and selling the products or services worldwide making a fortune. See yourself being interviewed by magazines and having articles written about you in newspapers. Write out in detail what your life is like in that future.

DAY 20

DANCING WITH ANGELS

Yesterday, you worked with building an avenue for the flow of your new money. You should be excited at your progress and proud of your ability to stick it through! Tomorrow will be three weeks. This is a good time to bring in the assistance of your guides, and guardians, of your Higher Self, of your Soul, to guide and assist you as you continue on this path. Your Higher Self also referred to as your Higher Consciousness is the highest, most consciously aware part of you. It is one of the best and greatest tools you have to assist you in this venture, but when it comes to money, it is a resource that is often overlooked or ignored. Why is that?

Money is often seen as the opposite of being spiritual. "Spiritual people have long hair, dirty robes, and sandals." "Spiritual people struggle to have enough money to pay their rent or their phone bills," but says the consensus, "It doesn't matter because they *are close to God*." Have you ever traced where these beliefs originated?

If you look at the history of Western religion, you'll see evidence of great wealth on the part of the Church. Grand, massive cathedrals,

DAY 20

beautiful altars of carved marble, priceless statues, paintings, solid gold bejeweled chalices, magnificent works of art created by the Great Masters: Michelangelo, De Vinci, Rubens, Rembrandt, Raphael, and Bellini. These items remain priceless possessions of churches across Europe and in many parts of the world. Clearly, it wasn't the churches that were poor only the masses of people who were told to sacrifice for the good of the whole.

On the opposite side of the spectrum are monks and priests who made vows of poverty and gave up all "worldly goods" devoting their time and energy to prayer and sacrifice. The belief that wealth and spirituality contradict each other has been around for thousands of years. Even Eastern religions speak of the importance of giving up "all earthy desires." Both extremes have developed through a history of chauvinism that has separated the world into divisions of either/or. Merriam-Webster's Dictionary defines money as:

> *something generally accepted as a medium of exchange, a measure of value, or a means of payment.*

Money is energy and it is a wonderful energy because it can be used in exchange for anything you want: a new house, a property on the beach, a vacation in Tahiti, a Lear Jet, a castle, a hotel, food, clothing, fuel for your car. All of these things can be purchased through this energy called money.

Hopefully, in your spiritual pursuits you have discovered a beautiful basis of spirituality. Perhaps you have connected with your Higher Self, or with guides, with your Soul, with your Spirit. Perhaps you've journeyed meditatively to ancient lands, met with Ancient Ones, Lemurian Dreamers, Archetypes, and other mystical friends. Yet the idea of money and spirituality remains distinctively separate. It's time to fill the gap.

In truth, everything you do in life is based on how open you are to receiving love and being loved. In this regard, you have, no doubt, done thousands of processes to heal your past and open to the future.

All of these steps lift you a little bit higher and open you a little bit more to being loved. Money is no different, but because it has such a bad rap, people often see it as bad. People judge wanting money as being greedy or selfish. People often judge others who have a lot of money as being unrelenting, uncaring, and unspiritual.

Yet, this energy of money, is part of the source of All That Is. It represents the ability to receive the unlimited, overwhelming bounty of this physical world. What could be more spiritual than that? Isn't that what you have been seeking? In truth, it is impossible to separate money from spirituality because they all originate from the same Source. Opening to receive requires acceptance as well as opening to the love which it represents. People who have great wealth may not have it all together. They may not always have successful relationships or perfect lives, but they have learned how to manifest and receive and the greater your level of receiving, the greater your ability to love and be loved. Opening to receive more money in your life is allowing yourself to open to receive on multiple levels!

It is imperative to alter the feelings you have around money and re-define what money represents. No doubt, you will agree that a loving father wants his children to have it all. A loving mother wants her sons and daughters to have everything that life can offer. This same level of love is available to you from God, from Goddess, from All That Is.

This is your final battle. In truth, it is the only battle. Opening to allow money to flow easily and effortlessly into your life, to allow it to flow abundantly, is the same energy that says you are worthy. You are loved. It is not all that there is or all that you will discover about love, but it is a wonderful opening to allow and receive. And it is long overdue.

DAY 20

The best part is your Higher Self, your Soul, your guides, and guardians will help you accomplish these goals. They will guide and support you in this endeavor. Your goal to manifest great wealth is simply a target of desire and because you desire it, you can allow yourself to reach and stretch beyond what limits you. Each time you receive more of whatever this planet has to offer, you receive a little more love. As you are discovering, releasing a belief that you don't deserve money, opens you to receive more love! Releasing a belief that you are not enough, doesn't just alter your ability to receive money, it alters your ability to receive anything. You are on more than a journey to just raise your finances; you are on the most spiritual endeavor of your life. Because, if you can succeed at this, you are opening to more and more love everywhere in your life, a love that gives you what you want. You are opening to a love that is in everything and your task is to learn to receive it!

Opening your heart to allow money to flow abundantly into your life, creates more peace and joy. You can flow this same peace and joy out into the world, helping the world to open to this same peace and joy. Money is an energy that can bring great happiness and provide solutions to so many problems and challenges in the world.

Your Higher Self, Soul, and Guides know the most perfect way for you to reach your goal of great wealth. They want you to succeed because they want you to achieve all that is possible, opening your heart to all the bounty that is available. In doing so, you are opening to a higher resonance of love, the ultimate goal in not just manifesting great bounty and happiness, but in living your life to the fullest.

When you pursue your dreams, it is more than just you at work. You've heard the phrase "you are not alone." Your Higher Self, Soul, and Guides are there with you as part of your expansion and desire to reach for more. They are right there by your side. This is what they want for your life and what they planned for you before you were even born. They know what you planned to accomplish and are with you to help you achieve those goals. They are tuned in to you. Now, it's time to tune in to them so you can hear, sense, and feel them in all you do, particularly now, when your goal is so clear and focused.

If you aren't accustomed to hearing their voice or to sensing their guidance, you miss out on so much of what they can give to you.

They are here to help you manifest all that you want in life. Open to their support and guidance. A relationship with your Soul, Spirit, Higher Self and guides is a powerful resource in your ability to manifest not only more money in your life, but to manifest anything. Include an enhanced relationship with your Higher Self, Guides, and Guardians as part of that bounty. Imagine being able to sense or hear them in all you do - learning to trust that sense as you make decisions in your life. By following the exercises in the section that follows, you can get skilled at this, building more confidence in yourself and your connection with them as well as trusting more and more in the messages you receive. Once they know you are listening and receiving what they have for you, they will jump on board, full speed ahead!

Tuning in to sense or hear your Higher Self and other unseen friends, is a skill that can be developed and improved with practice.

You may already have an ability to sense and receive guidance in your meditations and, in time, you can trust more and more that their guidance is available to you in your normal, daily life.

A great suggestion is to ask for support or guidance when you are not totally focused on getting the answers you need. What this means is, ask a question in your head while you are driving the car, taking the dog for a walk, or working on your computer. Present your question and then release it, waiting for the answer to come at a later point in time. The answer may come in many playful ways. Perhaps, you ask a question

DAY 20

and an hour or so later you hear the announcer on the television or the radio speaking words that respond to your request. Perhaps, you get a phone call that is exactly what you needed to hear or you receive an email or letter than provides the guidance you are seeking. You may even just get an intuitive sense or an *aha* that provides the answers you seek.

At first, you may doubt the answers. You may think you are just imagining it, but trust what you are sensing. In time, the answers will become clearer. The answers or guidance you receive from your Higher Self and Guides will be empowering, supportive, and loving.

Look for that in your day-to-day life. Watch for responses. Listen. Pay attention. Your Higher Self or Guides will get through if you are open to receive the messages. Write down what you hear or sense, particularly in the morning as you wake. Dreams can be particularly powerful ways to get messages through to you.

Try to be more and more present in the moment. When you are eating food, notice what you are eating. Enjoy each morsel. If you walk your dog, notice the grass, the flowers, the wind, and the sun. As you practice this, you will be of clearer mind. There will be less chatter and errant thoughts which will ultimately allow you to be more open to receive messages from your guides and Higher Self. As you clear the mental clutter from your mind, you are opening space for your Guides to reach through to you. Remember, they are with you all the time, but your ability to hear, sense, see, and know that they are there responding and guiding may be blocked or limited.

As you open these channels, your Higher Self and Guides can lead you to answers and activities that will bring you great wealth. There is no limit to the amount of abundance you can have and your Guides want you to have it. Abundance and over-flowing bounty is a natural state of your physical world. Everything on this planet is overflowing with abundance. Look at the number of stars in the sky, the grains of sand on the beach, the number of fish in the sea, the number of birds, trees, and flowers. There is evidence of an unending abundance everywhere you look. Yet you struggle with money. You may be in debt. You may have barely enough to get by or you may have just enough to be comfortable, but now you have a powerful resource that you can enhance and develop. As you are opening to more and more abundance in your life, you are allowing yourself to be loved in whole new ways. Your Higher Self has been waiting for ways to show you that you are loved and is thrilled to be an active part of your life. They are there for you 100%.

Use the exercises in the next section to practice new ways to receive support and guidance from your Higher Self and other unseen friends. Practice the exercises and, like any relationship, give it the time and attention it needs to build love and intimacy.

EXERCISE 20

RECEIVING SPIRITUAL SUPPORT AND GUIDANCE

In addition to your regular meditation work, use the following exercises to expand your awareness of your Higher Self, Guides and Guardians in your day-to-day life.

1. Make a list of at least 5 realistic, practical questions that you would like your Guides to answer. They can be questions such as, "why am I always struggling to have enough?" Or, "What can I do to break my limiting earning pattern?" Perhaps you want to know "why am I always in debt?" Then use any of the following techniques to get your answer. Write out what you discover.

> **Inner dialogue.** Carry on an inner dialogue with your Higher Self and Guides every day. Talk to them saying such things as "I know you are there. Please speak to me or show me a sign that you are there." Or, "Show me a sign of the best way I can generate more income today." Talk to them as you would talk to a friend. Know they are listening. Spend the rest of the day, looking for the answer to your question. You may just sense, intuit an answer. Sometimes, it may sound like the voice of someone you know speaking to you in your head. Sometimes, it may sound like the voice of logic or reason or of compassion. You may see wording written across the TV screen or a message on a license plate. Be open. Watch and listen. Messages from your Higher Self and Guides will never be negative or condescending, but are always positive and uplifting. In time, you will begin to trust more and more of what you are sensing or hearing. Write down in your notebook or journal whatever

you perceive to be an answer, no matter how small or unbelievable it may be. Be persistent. Answers will come!

Sit and Talk. Imagine you are in a beautiful garden or near a pond that has a wooden or stone bench. Ask your Higher Self and Guides to join you there so you can sit and chat. At first, it may feel like you imagined it, but in time it will become more and more real to you. Write down what you experience. Keep talking to this manifestation of your Higher Self or Guide until it feels like you are talking to someone real and the answers you're getting don't seem like they're coming from your own head. This can take time and practice.

Journaling. Journaling can be a wonderful and easy way to open a dialogue with your Guides. Use a computer or handwrite in a notebook. You can use the list of questions you wrote in number 1 above or you can start with an entirely new question. Write the question at the top of the first page. Then sense or listen for the answer and type or write it out. Then ask another question. Keep going. Even if at first it seems like you are speaking to yourself, keep practicing with the intention to go deeper. Before long you will notice a shift in the answers you get. Don't filter or try to figure it out. Just write out what you sense or hear. Sometimes beautiful, meditative music in the background can help set the mood while you're doing this and assist in raising your vibration.

Sensing Your Guide. Select a color that represents your Higher Self, Guide or Guardian to you. For example, let's say you select a pale violet or a light blue. Now spend the entire day looking for evidence of that color. When you see the color - no matter where that may be - know your Guides are responding to you, letting you know they are

EXERCISE 20

there for you. At first it may seem silly - a violet colored car or a purple house, but acknowledge and thank them for making their presence known to you. As time goes on, you will see greater and greater evidence that they are present everywhere in your life. Once you are feeling skilled at seeing them around you in your reality, start asking them questions. Start with simple ones and then expand to more complex ones as your confidence in your abilities increases.

As always, write what you discover in your notebook or journal.

DAY 21

GRATITUDE

Today is three weeks into this 30-day program. Congratulations for sticking with it. Over the last three weeks you've programmed a Statement of Desire. You've been exploring and releasing limiting beliefs. You've been working to reprogram your subconscious, expand your self-image, and are continuing to raise and hold your financial resonance. Yesterday, you connected in a powerful way with your Higher Self and Guides, who join with you in achieving your goal of great wealth.

By this time, you should be seeing evidence of improvements in your finances. As we discussed in prior weeks, there are essentially four major steps to manifesting anything you desire:

1. focus on what you want
2. build and hold the frequency of having it
3. give thanks and let it go
4. act as if you already have it

If you are not seeing any evidence of change in your financial reality at this point, then check the prior four steps. You know where you are strong and where you are weak. How specific is your goal? The more specific you are, the easier it is to focus. When you do that, you make it

DAY 21

more real and more possible. Get detailed on what you want so that you can focus specifically on achieving it.

The frequency building stage is the most important because your emotional state is your rocket fuel! If you want to get a rocket off the ground, you've got to really push hard until you get outside the atmosphere of resistance. Your emotions generate a powerful frequency that will lift you from where you have been all these years to where you want to be.

Step Three is saying thank you and releasing your desire to the Universe so it can come back to you. This is essentially the step of releasing the *what and when* while holding onto the desire and expectation. And, Step Four is taking action in your world to open an avenue for your new riches. All these steps are important. Don't skip any of them.

Today we are going to work On Step Three which is the letting go part, but it also includes a really powerful component: *Gratitude*.

Gratitude is a very powerful energy. It is about being thankful for everything you are creating through the exercises in this book, for everything you are creating in your life even the setbacks and disappointments. Because gratitude is an energy, it carries its own resonance and when added with your resonance and that of your desires and motivation for great wealth, it can be the very piece that carries your weak or low energy over the top.

Gratitude, like any energy, will replicate itself. Whatever you are truly grateful for will expand and grow. Gratitude can be a conscious tool you can use to bring in more and more abundance. It doesn't matter how small the thing may be, gratitude will make it expand. You know if you are feeling sorry for yourself, if you are blaming others, or seeing yourself as a victim, the resonance of those feelings will expand and grow creating more and more things to be sorry about, to blame others for, and to provide evidence that you really are a victim.

To have great wealth, you MUST be resonating on what it feels like to be wealthy. That's where the imagining comes in. You may not currently live in a mansion, but you can imagine you do. When you imagine living in a mansion, you expand what is possible. You open your mind to new possibilities. You lift your resonance to a new place and feel the excitement of what you imagine it feels like to be rich. The imaginings, in turn, trigger emotional responses of happiness, excitement, and joy, right? These are the energies that will bring in what you desire and then add on top of that the resonance of being appreciative and grateful for what you have! It's a powerful mix that will generate even more of what you are already creating.

As you look around today, Day 21 of this Money Magic Program, what do you see that you can be grateful for? Perhaps you just found a few coins on the sidewalk as you were walking the dog. It doesn't matter how much you found. It doesn't matter how big or small the manifestation may be, being grateful is going to lift that energy triple fold! You found a nickel. Say:

Thank You, Universe! I'm 5 cents richer than I was yesterday. I am grateful that my reality is responding to my goals and desires to have more money!

If you received a discount on something you purchased, be grateful for that. Be grateful for all the things in your life, including your health, good teeth, or great neighbors. Perhaps you have a car that keeps running and running, be grateful for having a car that is reliable. Be grateful for all that you have and all that you received today.

Being grateful allows you to appreciate others, but also yourself. Thank yourself for making the decision to purchase this book because it is showing you so much about who you are! Thank your Higher Self and Guides for responding to your requests. Thank your metaphysics for

DAY 21

giving you so much knowledge and magic. Embodying gratitude and practicing it in your daily life lifts you to a whole new frequency. You start focusing on the things that work in your life. You start noticing the wonderful things and people in your life that you might otherwise miss because you were so focused on what wasn't working. That can all change today! Here's the lesson for today:

> Every time you receive any evidence of money or abundance in your life, STOP AND AFFIRM: *I Am So Very Grateful for All the Money and Abundance That Continually Comes Into My Life.*

Children are wonderful with expectation. Most often, they see the world as overflowing with possibilities. Everything around them is fascinating, exciting and possible. If you tell a young child they are becoming very rich and that every day they will see evidence of this coming true, they will discover abundance at every turn. "Look, Momma, I found a penny!" "Look, Poppa, I found a bird feather." "Momma, that man put a quarter in the electric horse and let me ride."

Children in their innocence, do not hinder their excitement and enthusiasm at the prospect of having something more. If you tell them something will be, they believe it without a doubt. You can be this way too. It is a matter of where you put your focus and attention. Each daily event can be a reminder of the financial abundance you are attracting. You, the powerful manifester that you are, have unlimited ability to create and manifest anything you focus upon! As you continue to hold and build your excitement of wealth - KNOWING IT IS HAPPENING - use the energy of gratitude to accelerate your excitement. All you need to do is set an intention to feel grateful for any money or new things coming to you each day! If you have bills coming in, say thank you to your bills knowing you always come out okay, even in the worst of times. Everyone has a bottom line of how low they will fall. In the worst times of your life, you only fell so far. You still managed to have food, water and shelter. Remind yourself that you always come out okay and that you can turn even the worst events around. You've done it in the past and will do it again. How do you do that, by your intention and focus!

Being grateful for what you have and what you are continuing to build and receive is a habit you can develop. It will get stronger and easier over time as you remind yourself to look for what you do have that is bringing you closer to your ultimate goal. There are opportunities everywhere. Even finding a bird feather, can be a sign of abundance. Native American's perceive feathers as gifts from the sky. Everything you see, experience, and receive in a day can be seen as a *gift from the sky!*

Step Three of manifesting is releasing the desire for what you want while holding the expectation that it will return at the right time. Also, included in this step is being thankful, appreciative, and grateful for all you have. Thanking the Universe for bringing opportunity to you. Thanking the Universe in advance for responding to your requests. When you can feel this gratitude in your heart, it opens you to receive more love in your life. It lifts your resonance so you can move past negative emotions and allow money to start flowing to you. A state of gratitude allows the abundance you desire to pour into your life.

As we discussed yesterday, your Higher Self, Guides, Soul, and Spirit are supporting you in all your dreams and goals. No matter how bad things may seem financially, opening your heart from a space of gratitude will open doors. You will be guided and the way will be clear for the next step you need to take.

As you feel gratitude for what you have and for what you are creating, also allow yourself to trust. That is the purpose of the step of releasing. You are resonating on your ability to manifest all you desire. You are filled with expectation. You release the desire, KNOWING it will come back to you. You trust that you have done enough. You are Loved. You

DAY 21

are being guided and supported! Trust with all your being that you will receive what you asked for and MORE! Trust and live each day as though what you have requested is already here.

Every time you spend money, no matter what you buy, thank it for the service it is providing to you. Bless it for all the things you get in exchange for money: food, electricity, water, a beautiful home, a car, fuel for your car, even the bills in your business that allow your business to grow and thrive. Money is a source of energy that is used "in exchange" for things. The more money you have, the more you can spend, so be grateful for all you spend as well!

As you are doing the exercises, meditations, and visualizations, and resonating on the riches you desire, you are creating an abundance consciousness. Adding gratitude to the energies you are already generating will enhance your desires and lift your expectations. There is a side bonus too. All this work will lift your spirits. You will be much happier. You are consciously lifting your resonance. You are richer - financially, emotionally and spiritually.

EXERCISE 21

IMPLEMENTING GRATITUDE

1. Write in your journal or notebook, a list of things you are thankful for in your life. At first, it may seem like a feeble exercise and the list may seem short, but as you continue doing this exercise each day, you will notice that you are turning your focus and attention toward finding things that you appreciate in your life. Make this a daily exercise and you will see the benefits.

2. Choose a sum of money that you would like to receive in the next few weeks. Make it a small sum that you believe you can reasonably manifest in a short time. Write the amount on a piece of paper or 3 x 5 card and set it somewhere where you will see it regularly throughout your day. Place it on the refrigerator, on the bathroom mirror, on the TV or next to your bed. Then look at it several times a day, imagining you have received the exact amount you have written. Focus on the feeling of gratitude and sense how grateful you will feel when the money does arrive. After you do the exercise, go on with your day, releasing the goal until the next time you focus on what you've written on the card. Write out what you experience.

3. In this exercise, you will focus on something you already have that you deeply appreciate and feel grateful to have in your life. Perhaps it is a special pet, a piece of jewelry, your home or car, a job you love or a good friend. Throughout the day, think about how grateful you are to have this in your life. Think about how happy this person or thing makes you feel and repeat out loud the following words:

Thank you for blessing me with your presence in my life. I am so grateful to have this. I feel blessed! Thank you! Thank you!

EXERCISE 21

Do this several times a day, and you'll definitely feel some good things happening! Use your journal to write out your experiences.

DAY 22

ROUNDING THIRD

You're now rounding the bend, heading to the finish line of this 30 day program. Your new wealth identity doesn't stop at the end of this course. Nor is this a time to quit or even slow down. This last week should be the most intense of the four weeks. You've been working diligently with beliefs, creating new ones while releasing those that don't serve you. You've stretched your image and are continuing to do so. The goal isn't to lift just a little bit, but to maintain a whole new identity creating a new lifestyle of great riches. During these last eight days, you will need to work harder than you've even done before. As Arnold Schwarzenegger said about achieving his title of Mr. Olympia (seven times):

> *"There's no maybe. You've gotta get up and say I'm going to be a champion. You need to do whatever it takes."*

After three weeks, the challenge is to keep the resonance going. It's easy to lose momentum, particularly if you are not manifesting any changes in your financial state. If that is the case, there are two things to evaluate at this point:

DAY 22

1. Why isn't your level of manifesting increasing, and
2. What can you do to lift and maintain a higher level of excitement?

As you know, the whole key to manifesting anything in life is vibration. This planet is 100% energy. Everything in it, including thoughts, feelings, desires, expectations, even your imagination, has a vibrational frequency. Everything in your current life has a vibrational frequency from your physical body to your house and, of course, your money pattern. Over the last three weeks, you have become aware of your beliefs around money, your fears of having more, your money image, and the pattern of earning you've been holding in place since you were a child. Hopefully, you've been doing the exercises and using the various techniques to change whatever it is that is holding you back. So, let's look at why your reality is staying the same.

1. **Honesty.** First, of course, is to be honest about the effort you've put in to reaching your goal. As we said on Day 4 - you must have a *burning desire* to reach your goal. A few days ago, we talked about motivation and included inspirational thoughts and quotes from highly successful people. Every single one of them says you must set your sight on a goal and NEVER QUIT. If you're motivation to alter your money pattern is weak, you won't be able to lift out of a pattern that's been locked in place for decades. So, how do you lift your motivation? Use the tools we have been providing such as visualizing what it feels like to have things you truly desire, changing your self-image, connecting with the power of the future, and stepping into the Circle of Abundance. Find any resistances and release them. Get excited again by working with your belief of what's possible!

2. **Focus**. Realize that it is expected that your desire and expectation will wane. That is a natural part of living on this physical plane. If you

find yourself slipping back to the same old pattern of the past, forgive yourself, and rev up again! Hold your focus and keep going. Focus is such an important tool to achieving your goals. It is more important than self-discipline, more important than willpower, and more important than even motivation itself, because if you can maintain your focus, you will always achieve your goal! But, even with only one goal, maintaining focus can be difficult. It's, therefore, important to find ways to keep your focus on your goal. Here's some ideas that may help:

- ✓ Read as much as possible about your goal, on websites, blogs, in books or magazines
- ✓ Post notes or reminders on your refrigerator, computer, and bathroom mirror - places where you will see them throughout your day
- ✓ Send yourself reminders from an online calendar
- ✓ Do a visualization or meditation every morning just as you wake up and each night before you fall asleep
- ✓ Create affirmations that you repeat to yourself throughout your day to reinforce accomplishing each goal
- ✓ Regularly write in a notebook or journal about your goals and the events in your day that were successful
- ✓ Make a list at the end of each day of at least five things that occurred for which you are grateful

All the exercises, affirmations, visualizations, and meditations in this book are designed to support and maintain your focus and to lift your resonance to the level of what it feels like to have what you want! Use these tools to keep your excitement up. YOU WILL ACHIEVE your goal!

2. **Expectation.** Expectation is the biggest challenge in building and

DAY 22

maintaining your new money resonance. Of all the creation tools, this is the one that is the most powerful and the one that falters most often. When your expectation is weak or lacking, other energies will take its place. Instead of knowing that what you have put in motion will come to be, you doubt or worry and feel anxious or you just plain refuse to believe it is possible. All these things are evidence of faltering expectation.

Of course, this is a challenge. You can imagine having a check for $200,000 in your hand and you can desire it, but if your expectation is that it will never happen or even that you "hope" that maybe it will, that is not sufficient to bring about the change you want in your life. Your current reality is in place because of the expectations you currently hold. Those expectations are so solid and so fixed that you may not even know they exist. But, think about it for a moment. What is your current money situation? You always have enough? That's an expectation. It prevents you from having more than enough. If your current reality is that as soon as you have enough, it will be taken away, then that is exactly what will happen. So instead of expecting the new reality, you expect what you've always had.

Expectations flow from your emotions and underlying beliefs that support those emotions and play a critical role in your ability to manifest what you want. You always have an expectation of some sort. It just may not be what you say you want.

It is important to know what beliefs are behind your expectation or lack of it. Do you expect to fail at achieving your money goals? If so, it will come to pass. Do you expect that you will make a few changes, but then everything will go back to the way it was? That too will come to pass. To change expectations, you must get to the bottom of the emotions and beliefs that support them. You've been working with beliefs. What beliefs support an expectation of failure? Have you failed in the past, so you expect to fail again? Why is that true and what beliefs do you have to support that conclusion? Find the beliefs and clear them out. Work with your expectation so that it is solid and truly supportive of what you want to achieve.

On prior pages, we've discussed the importance of building your resonance of how great it feels to be wealthy. You initially set a goal in a written Statement of Desire with instructions to read it twice a day. If you stopped doing that, or lost the paper, then start over again. Re-write it and review it at least twice a day! You also selected a smaller, more achievable goal with the intention of building your excitement and enthusiasm around money. You are putting your natural tools of desire, imagination, and expectation into action using your imagination to inspire and expand your desire and using your expectation to hold onto the belief that you will get what you want.

The best way to maintain a high resonance is to continue doing what you know to do - imagine what it feels like to have what you want and not to let go of it. This doesn't have to be a logical endeavor. If you have determined that you want $100,000 by New Year's Day, hold that intention! Don't worry about how it will happen, just work to build your expectation that it will! As stated above, keep reminders all over your house, your office, even in your car so you remember you are GOING TO HAVE $100,000 BY NEW YEARS DAY! Repeat this goal inside your head throughout the day by creating a verbal mantra such as "I am a multi-millionaire" or "I'm getting $100,000 in January."

Remember, your current reality of lack or mediocrity or even of being in debt is held in place because that is what you expect it to be. You can change your expectation. You can change your beliefs. Do that and get back to reminding yourself repeatedly of what you are creating. See it as happening now and, most importantly, keep the emotional energy generating as continuously as possible because that is what will ultimately bring in the success you desire. It is also that energy that will

DAY 22

hold and maintain your success once you accomplish it!

If, on the other hand, you find that you're not motivated to keep going, then be honest with yourself and accept the fact that where you are at is where you want to be! You are creating your financial situation right now and tomorrow and the next day. If you want to change it, if you want to lift this rocket off the ground to a new level, then you must work to get there. It's not about easing up and "hoping" it will come to be. You either create it or you don't. It's up to you. If you want it. You can do it.

"Whatever the mind can conceive and believe, it will achieve!"
--- Napoleon Hill

EXERCISE 22

BUILDING EXPECTATION

1. Motivation letter. Imagine your closest and dearest friend is reading this book and getting very discouraged and thinking of giving up. Write them a heartfelt letter of all the reasons they should not give up. Fill the letter with as much emotion as you can engender. Do everything you can think of to convince them to keep going and not to quit.

2. **Focusing.** What is the first thing you want to do with your new found money? Perhaps it is to buy a new car or even pay off the car you have. Or, perhaps it is to manifest a certain sum of money. Focus on this very specific goal and write out answers to each of the following questions:

a. What is the specific item or thing you want to manifest first?

b. When do you expect you will be able to create this item or thing actually happening in your life? Be realistic as to what you believe is possible, for example, within 1 year or next month or by December 1st.

c. Write down several options of how you expect this thing will occur? For example, do you obtain a bank loan? Do you receive a check in the mail? Do you enter into a successful contract that provides you more money than you expected? Someone gives you what you want as a surprise? Write out every option that is possible, no matter how remote.

d. On a scale of 1-10, what is the level of your expectation that this goal will be achieved within the time period you have set?

EXERCISE 22

e. Write out detailed reasons why you think your expectation is anything less than a 10 and what you believe you need to do to lift it higher.

f. What needs to happen for you to believe that this thing you expect is absolutely going to happen, *i.e.*, a level 10 expectation?

DAY 23

WHO YOU ARE BECOMING

In alignment with prior discussions on shifting image, we're going to expand the idea of developing your new wealth character. Great actors and writers know that to make a character "real" you have to give them both depth and dimension. Award winning actors and story tellers bring in as much detail as possible about a character. Matthew McConaughey, for example, spent six months preparing for his role as an anti-gay, misogynist in *Dallas Buyer's Club*. He lost 47 pounds and locked himself indoors for months so his skin would get pale and pasty and he could better understand the emotional pains of his character. In immersing himself into the character he was about to play, he transformed his entire image, taking on the mannerisms, expressions, and attitudes of the person he was going to portray. As a result, he was awarded the highest of honors, an Academy Award for Best Actor in 2013.

Our goal in this section is to bring your millionaire character to life. You've been told again and again that the way to manifest what it is you desire, becoming a person of great wealth, is to make that new identity as real as your current one. To do this, to add depth, and dimension, you need to get into the details of the character you want to become.

What makes a character great in any novel or film? Great characters

DAY 23

stick in your memory because there is something remarkable about them that you never seem to forget. It's more than just a hero or heroine in a story. Such characters are real. They have a vulnerability about them, qualities we admire and what often makes them the most real is that they are flawed. To develop a truly memorable character, you must put as much of yourself into the role as you can, but you must also make this character, soulful and alive, filled with the vibrancy of life. You create this character out of your imagination, making them as real as possible and then, the actor that you are, steps into this character and breathes life into them making them someone that no one will ever forget.

What does a great actor have to do to convince their audience that the character they are playing is real? They explore and discover the character's quirks, habits, and eccentricities. They study and rehearse the character's mannerisms whether that be looking admiringly in the mirror or tapping a pen on the end of a table. They study the character's speech pattern, voice pitch, and mimic their posture until the mannerisms feel real and natural. Great scripts often include a "backstory" on each character so the actors can further glean the character's personality and emotional history. Understanding where the character comes from and what challenges they have met in their life adds depth and realness.

McConaughey's role in Dallas Buyer's Club was based on a real person. Though no longer alive, McConaughey was still able to learn about the character by doing research on him. He read books, newspaper articles, notes, and papers written by the person he was to portray. He spoke to people who knew the person, all the while searching for clues and information on how to BE this person in every detail. He knew what brand of alcohol the character drank, whether he liked coffee or not, what kind of clothes he wore, and the kind of friends and family he had. He dove deeply into the inner psyche of the character so that he could do more than act, but could become this person!

With the same detail and intensity, you can discover and develop the millionaire that you strive to be. You can step into the mindset of this character and become as intimate with it as you are with your current self. You can practice and rehearse the role with such detail and precision that this character's words, thoughts, and actions are not just who you pretend to be, but become who you are. If actors can do this, you can do it as well. You don't need to take acting classes or study great plays or scripts. You only need a burning desire to become this person - inhaling every thought, every scent, and every touch until you are this person through and through.

For the next few days, we will work to develop a character you can become and you can play. You can develop every aspect of the person you desire to be and write the script with such detail and truth that you know this new person inside and out.

Great acting moves and touches people because it brings forth something so real that no one dares to doubt it. Great acting is filled with Soul and inspired by Spirit that sets the stage on fire and touches and moves the audience. That is great acting and you are going to become the greatest actor of all time. The stage is your world and the story is your life.

To develop your character, you must have an idea of who you want this character to be. You know this person is incredibly rich, but what else do you know about them? To play this character with any realness you need to believe in the character and know that it fits with who you already are. Though you may not want to emulate Gordon Gekko (*Wall Street*) or Lex Luthor (*Superman*), there are many characters, both real and fictional that can be the inspiration for your new self. Go online and find a list of the wealthiest people in the world and select one you want to model for development of your goal character.

Select someone who is extremely wealthy so you can study them,

DAY 23

learn all about them, and begin to see, and eventually emulate, - the qualities of this person that makes them a success. There are numerous resources on the internet for you to be able to learn about nearly anyone. Very wealthy, successful people are not as private as perhaps they'd like to be. One of the best resources you will find is any of the online video channels, YouTube, Vimeo, Google Video, or TED Talks, because in video, you are not only listening to what they have to say, but you can learn about their mannerisms, dress style, personality quirks, and other things that tell you about their inner world. That is what you want to explore and discover. Do your research on this person and then write down what you have learned about their communication style, how they talk, what mannerisms they use. What kind of family background do they come from? And most importantly what beliefs do you think they have?

The exercises in the next few pages will help you detail these qualities so you can begin to emulate your new money mentor and become as wealthy as they are!

EXERCISE 23

DEVELOPING CHARACTER

In this exercise, you are going to begin by selecting someone in your world who is extremely wealthy so you can study them, learn all about them and begin to see - and eventually emulate - the qualities of this person that makes them such a success. They may be someone you already know and, if not, there are numerous resources on the internet for you to be able to learn about nearly anyone. Search on YouTube or Vimeo for videos of this person or of several people until you select the one you want to emulate. You may find interviews, speeches, news stories that will help you get to know this person inside out. Notice mannerisms, dress style, personality quirks. Listen to what they say to glean how they think and operate on a personal level. Do your research on this person and then answer the following questions in as much detail as possible.

1. Name. Write the name of the person you want to model:

2. Communication style. How do they talk? Do they favor certain words or phrases that make them distinct and interesting? Listen to the sound of their voice. Much of our personality comes through our speech, so think about the way your character talks. What about their style of communication is distinctive and unique?

3. History. Where do they come from? What events shaped their personality? What did his or her father do for a living? How about mother? How many siblings do they have? What kind of family background do they have? (Loving, supportive, abusive, dysfunctional...?) What events led this person to their career choices?

EXERCISE 23

4. Appearance. Describe their physical appearance in detail. How do they dress? What kind of clothing? How interested are they in fine clothing? How about hair style?

5. Relationships. What kind of friends and family do they have? How do they relate to them? Are they social or reclusive, or somewhere in between? People can be defined by the company they keep, so this is a good way to define their character.

6. Ambition. What is his or her passion in life? What goal are they trying to accomplish? What is their unrecognized, internal need and how do they meet that need?

7. Thoughts. What kind of internal dialogue do you imagine this person has? How do they think through problems and dilemmas? If they hit a conflict in life, how do you expect they will handle it?

8. **Beliefs.** What beliefs do you think they have?

9. **Values.** Describe their values.

10. **Qualities.** Describe the qualities you think this person has.

11. **Perspectives.** Summarize their perspectives on life.

12. **Relate.** How much do you relate to this person? What qualities do they have that you have as well and vice versa?

Taking the list of information you gathered above, write a paragraph about this person, their talents, strengths, and abilities and what it is about them that makes them such a mega-success (and ultra-wealthy.)

DAY 24

MODELING

If you did yesterday's exercise, you should have discovered some interesting qualities about the millionaire (or billionaire) you selected as your mentor/model. You may have also discovered that you have many of those same qualities. Perhaps you are also adventurous, responsible and playful. Perhaps you also love to create new things, love people, and are a visionary.

As you go deeper into this exploration, there are some qualities you may want to build upon, perhaps others you may want to eliminate. The mentor you selected is not perfect in all things, but they have some specific traits that have made them super-successful and we want to discover what those are.

In prior exercises, you learned that wealthy people think quite differently than poor or middle class people. They have different ways of looking at life. They raise their children with different values and beliefs about money than the average person. You've been encouraged to let go of limiting beliefs about money and to stretch your imagination about what is possible. A great way to do that is to hang out with a multi-millionaire and get to know what they do, how they think, and why they do what they do.

DAY 24

You can go online and discover the current list for the some of the world's wealthiest people. Notice the areas in which many of them have worked to create great wealth. Though some of these people inherited their wealth, the majority of them have created their own success, many starting with nothing. These individuals are grand models for success. They have very specific qualities, beliefs, values, and perspectives on life that you can emulate. Wouldn't it be fascinating to step into the mind of someone like Bill Gates, Warren Buffet, or Oprah Winfrey and see how they think and get an idea of what they do differently that has resulted in such great wealth and success?

In the 1930's, Napoleon Hill published one of the most read books ever written called *Think and Grow Rich*. This book was the result of 25 years of interviewing and studying the wealthiest men in the western world. Similarly, in more recent years, author Steven Siebold spent nearly 30 years interviewing the wealthiest people in the world. They both discovered, as have many others, that extremely wealthy people have a different value system and a different way of viewing life. They have different strategies for creating success and for the enjoyment of life than non-wealthy people. To get an idea of how they think differently, see *How Rich People Think* at the end of this text. *(Appendix III.)*

As a result of such studies, therapists and self-growth gurus have studied the personalities of these exceptional people with the goal of modeling their behavior. Tony Robbins is one of the most successful at using these techniques. In fact, back in the late 90's, he modeled army sharp shooters so effectively that after only a few days of observation and practice, his skills were as good as expert sharp shooters with years of experience! How did he do it? He got intimately familiar with more than just the skills of sharp shooting, but how the experts walk, how they talk, how they see things in their mind; how they talk to themselves in their head and how they think. Essentially, he learned their inner strategies for doing the tasks they do and, as a result, he became expert at the same tasks in an extremely short period of time. What he did is called *modeling,* a superior form of learning that is extremely powerful.

Modeling is something everyone knows how to do. As children, many of the things you learned were based on modeling someone else's behavior. You learned how to use a spoon or tie your shoes by modeling what your parents or older siblings showed you. The key to modeling is based on two things, observing and mapping the successful processes that another uses in the actions you want to mimic. The key to modeling in this program is observing and mapping the processes that create exceptional results and monetary success. In other words, you find someone who is ridiculously good at making money and then you follow their steps, mimicking exactly what they do to bring about those same results.

To improve your chances of creating the great wealth you desire, you will begin by copying the gestures of an extremely wealthy, successful person of your choice. Physical gestures are a good start to emulating this successful person, but physical gestures are only part of the secret. To truly master someone else's skills, you need to also master their inner workings, their beliefs, their strategies, all the thought processes that underlie their skills and behaviors.

Modeling is different than traditional learning. In traditional learning, the goal is to master a skill by learning how to *do* something. You repeat the same steps or procedures again and again. You make adjustments in the *doing* of the process and you practice that *doing* over and over again. In modeling, however, it is far more important to determine the *being* of the person who has successfully developed and demonstrated that skill. In modeling, your focus is on each element of the model's behavior, to find the secret essential to their success.

Yesterday, you made a list of noticeable qualities, behaviors, and traits

DAY 24

of a very wealthy, successful person who you want to model. As you observed them or read about them, you were able to glean deeper qualities such as what drives them as well as their values and their beliefs. You learned these things based on listening to what they have to say as well as observing how they see the world and the way they participate in certain activities.

Richard Branson, for example, is a very casual, seemingly shy kind of guy, but he has a zest for life, a passion for adventure, and will go for a challenge every time. Though he appears somewhat uncomfortable facing an audience or even looking an interviewer in the eye, he has no problem jumping out of an airplane, parasailing, or climbing a mountain. What kind of behavioral patterns does this demonstrate? His success with over 200 companies shows he loves to create new things and trusts others to follow his vision. He is not afraid to go for it even if the odds may not be in his favor. By studying this man, you can get ideas about his personality that move him to success. He is humble yet daring. He is modest yet passionate and open to explore and experience anything new. What qualities do you have that are similar? What is the difference between the way you approach life and challenges and the way that Richard Branson does? Write down your answers in your journal or notebook.

EXERCISE 24

HOW TO MODEL BEHAVIORS

Imagine you are interviewing the person you selected as your mentor. Get into a deep rapport with your money mentor and imagine what they say to each question below, writing out the answer to each.

1. "How do you come up with an idea for a new business?"

2. "When you come up with a new idea, what's the first thing you do to implement the idea?"

3. "What's the next thing you do?"

4. "Do you do any pre-testing to see if this idea will be successful or not?"

5. "At what point do you decide that this is something you want to pursue?"

6. "Are there any specific things you look for in making a determination that this idea will be successful or not?"

7. "When you make the decision that this is something you want to pursue, what do you do next?"

8. "Once you make a decision that this is a business you want to build, how much effort do you put into the new venture?"

9. When you are implementing a new venture, how do you know that it will be financially successful?" "Is there a point where you decide that it is an idea that will not be profitable? If so, explain how you know when you have reached that point":

EXERCISE 24

10. "If you were going to teach me to become a multi-millionaire, what would you want me to know?"

11. "What skills do you have that enable you to create immense wealth?"

12. "How did you learn how to do this?"

13. "What do you believe about yourself when you do this?"

14. "How do you know that you're good at making money?"

15. "When you are building a new idea into a success, what emotional and physical state are you in when you do this?"

16. "Why do you think you are so good at making money?"

Imagine you are observing your money mentor doing what they normally do to make money. Perhaps you are at their office or place of business. Perhaps you are sitting in their home office, observing them perform a sequence of actions at their highest level of excellence. There is no one else in the room. Watch and listen to everything they do and say. Write what you observe about them and anything you hear them say.

Imagine you step inside of this person looking through their eyes and listening through their ears. Imagine this person is operating at their highest level of excellence. Describe in detail how do you feel as you do this. Repeat this exercise several times and write down everything you observe and experience in your journal.

Imagine you are involved doing something you are extremely good at doing (or have been good at doing.) Imagine you are at a distance observing yourself doing this particular activity or skill. Write down what you notice about your physical actions and movements.

1. What do you notice about your gestures?
2. Describe how you walk.
3. Describe how you talk.
4. Describe your level of focus.

Write out what you think about as you are doing these activities.

1. What feelings do you feel?
2. What is your attitude as you do this activity?
3. Write what you sense and observe about your own state of excellence?
4. Compare what you do and how you do things to the person you've selected as your model of excellence.

Create a picture in your mind of you doing a particular activity where you excel and then answer the following questions:

1. How far away is the image?
2. Is the image in color or is it black and white?
3. When you see this image, where is it located? High? Low? Left? Right?

Double the size of the picture and double it again. Keep doing that until it fills your whole vision. You are now in the zone. In that frame of mind, think about what you want to create and how you plan on doing it. Write your observations and experiences in your journal.

DAY 25

YOUR NEW SCRIPT

Did you do the exercises yesterday to get intimate with the inner workings of the millionaire you selected as your money mentor? If so, you should have already learned a great deal about this person and how they think when it comes to creating success and great wealth.

You may also imagine that you step into the mind of this person so you can really feel and sense how they think and feel! What do you discover?

Today, we are going to take what you learned and turn it into a new script; a new life script that you can live within from this day forward. In this script, you design the set, the setting, and the characters as well as the theme of the story. Just like a real movie, you create a feeling in the story to evoke an emotional response from the viewers. And like a movie script, the story can be ANYTHING you want it to be, but the main character of this story is YOU. You are the hero or heroine. This hero/heroine already has some amazing qualities and traits that make them unique for this story. Over the last few days, you got to know your mentor from the inside out so you can pull together all your best qualities and integrate them with this model of great success!

DAY 25

It is much easier to see yourself when you watch a movie because you don't get caught up emotionally in your thoughts or in the events that are happening. When you watch a movie, you empathize with the character despite their flaws and mistakes. You root for them. You want them to succeed, but most particularly, you can see the way out. You can see the big picture which perhaps they are struggling to find.

You are the hero of this new story, but you are also the author. You can write it any way you like, still giving the main character challenges to handle, but giving them the assistance they need to rise above each challenge. Like any Superhero, this character has unique and powerful qualities. They have positive values and traits so even in the worst of times, they find a way to come out on top! That's what makes a great story. You, as the hero of this story, have your own unique strengths along with unique talents and abilities, and in this new story, you are going to be called upon to use them. When you see yourself as the hero of your story you can perceive yourself differently. You can integrate the positive qualities you gleaned from the wealthy mentor you selected, blending those qualities with your own. Who is this new person you are discovering?

What is so exciting about this process is it can really change how you see yourself and how you feel! It also connects you to a positive future so you don't have to make any major shifts or changes to reach this new you. The smallest of changes in the present take you on an entirely new trajectory! Because the future is creating this present you only need to see and sense what lies ahead and it will pull you to it!

In your new story, you have triumphed over great adversity. This character comes from a troubled past. His or her parents were essentially flawed, filled with hubris or rage, a demand for perfection or their own incredible shame. Because they didn't know any better, they dumped their shame on you and you've been carrying it ever since. As a child growing up, you learned to cope. You developed strategies that work, perhaps fading into the background and hiding, perhaps martyring yourself, or pushing your demands on others so they won't see how truly fearful you are. These strategies get you through the rough times, but still feeling flawed and defective, you may feel you don't fit in, but you keep going, because that is who you are.

Flashbacks in this movie show a child standing on the playground watching the other kids play with a look of sadness or grief on their face. This child gets stronger though, despite the arguing at home; despite the events of pain, loss, despair. They keep going and move beyond the pain and disappointment.

Another flashback shows a vulnerable, dreamy eyed teen. You can see the beauty in this child, not yet an adult. They have amazing qualities that you, the viewer can see, even if this teen fails to see it. There is a strength in them that is inspiring. They have a drive and a determination that is extraordinary. They have a powerful imagination, a sense of power, and a capacity to dream. Another flashback shows this teen looking up to the sky reaching for their dreams. They look blissful, dreamy, believing they can do anything, but then, something terrible happens. The dream shatters. They fall. They crumble under the shattered dreams and disappointment. As a young teenage boy or girl, they are devastated and barely pick themselves up. You root for them. "*Get up! Get Up!*" They get up. You are so proud. This is the winner you know.

Then years pass. Your hero creates a nice life for himself or herself. They find a career and a partner they love. Perhaps, they get married and have children. Things are good! They've been able to put their past wounds behind them. They are living an okay life, not an extraordinary one, and you see again, there is such power and strength in the hero of your story. No matter how rough things get, they find a way to keep going. They suffer losses, betrayals, and heart breaks, but they have a determination that is inspiring. They have a light that glows no matter

DAY 25

how dim the world may seem around them. They discover a beautiful spirituality that lifts them and helps them to heal the pains of their past. You see this hero has so much more to give.

There is a challenge in this story. Something is happening that challenges your hero. It is not enough to just be okay. It is not enough to just be ordinary, but they don't see it. They don't see their talents, their skills, their unique strengths. They've learned to live an ordinary life because it is safe. Yet, there is something that calls to them to step up and be all they can be. That is the scene you are going to write next. Perhaps they are standing on a mountain top and realize they can have it all! Perhaps they are on the brink of change and must make a choice of which way will they go. Is there a sidekick that encourages them to keep going?

Don't give up now! You've come too far! It's time to make that pivotal choice. You need to let go of who they said you were and embrace who you truly are! It's time!" says the side kick.

You watch your hero shift both physically and emotionally. They stand and look to the sky. They feel a call and must respond because that is who they are. You see a look on their face that shows something is happening. Something is changing them. You know they get it.

You are loved! You are enough! You are so important to this world."

Your hero makes a new choice. Imagine the music in the background. It is triumphant! What is the new choice they make? What do that do that allows them to triumph over all past adversity.

Yes, there will be challenges, but I can do it! I know who I am and nothing is holding me back. Nothing can stop me now. This is who I truly am!

See this person embracing all the characteristics of the model of excellence you've been discovering through your mentor. See them smiling and laughing as they enjoy life! See them turning their dreams into reality. What are they doing? Teaching? Healing? Inspiring? Leading?

Make this dream huge. See them teaching masses of people; healing thousands; inspiring millions. How do they do it? Do they write books? Enter politics? Do public speaking? Create a business empire?

See this new "you" being interviewed just like you saw your mentor being interviewed. See how others are now watching you, as this hero, talking of your successes, asking you about your philosophy on life, your values and goals, and how you always succeed. Study this person now, just like you studied your mentor and glean all their inner workings. How do they think? What do they feel? How do they move, talk, and walk? See them for the leader they are, how they trust others to build the vision they have set in motion. Step into this character and live their life now! You've done it! You are here!

Write out what you discovered in your notebook or review the exercises below. Embrace what you have learned and discovered.

EXERCISE 25

WRITING YOUR NEW SCRIPT

On a blank sheet of paper, write out the following exercises:

1. The setting of your script is 5 years in the future. You are narrating your own story. You met the challenges described above and you triumphed. You've integrated the qualities of your mentor. You are now living an incredible life of great success and wealth. You are extremely happy, surrounded by people who love, admire, and respect you and are looking forward to the "what's next" opportunity. Write your story. You have triumphed. Write the story of how you got here as the narrator talking about your life and the journey that takes you to this incredible place of success and riches that you now are enjoying. Below is a sample you can copy and continue writing your story.

EXT - HAWAII - BACK PATIO - OCEAN FRONT ESTATE - MID-DAY

Two young boys are playing cards on the patio.

NARRATOR:

When I started on this journey I had no idea what I would do that would get me here. In fact, my dream to be a multi-millionaire has resulted in far more than I ever thought possible. It all goes back to that day in July when I made a firm decision that I was going to change my life for the better. Particularly, I decided I was going to change my financial future....

2. Following the guidelines described above, re-write the story of your past. Change the significance of the incidents and through them see your unique powers and strengths. See yourself triumphant!

3. Imagine you are in an amazing future, where you are as wealthy and successful as the mentor you selected. See how others are now watching you - as this hero - talking of your successes, your philosophy on life, your values and goals, and how you always succeed. Write out what you discover.

DAY 26

FEAR STAND-OFF

Today is Day 26 - only four more days of this 30 day program. A lot has been covered and yet, for many, nothing changes. You know if your motivation is weak. You know if you are doing the work or not, but what if you are reading every chapter and doing every exercise and things still seem stagnant? This can be true of anything you want to manifest. You set the intention, focus on manifesting it, release it to the Universe and then return to the same ol' same ol'. Why doesn't your intention manifest as you desired?

The sole reason that something does not manifest as you intend is because your personal, vibrational frequency does not match the frequency of what you desire. Without realizing it, there's a pattern in place that says NOT to manifest what you say you want. We discussed this conflict on Day 14, addressing two parts that have opposing goals. There is one that wants you to have great wealth, but another part says "no," perhaps even saying "absolutely not." It is clearly important to integrate these conflicting parts, but if you did the integrating parts exercise and are still not manifesting what you desire, there is something more powerful operating underneath. Sometimes, it may show as sabotage. You create money coming in and then screw up the whole

DAY 26

program, get in an argument with your boss or spouse. Perhaps you create a great success and then end up being abandoned and punished by someone you love. It's not the form that is important, but the pattern and the emotion that is holding it in place.

There are many transformational leaders and teachers that promote change based on either the principle of gaining pleasure or of avoiding of pain. Everyone has developed strategies for dealing with both. Often, these strategies are not logical because they are based on old conclusions and beliefs formed when you were an illogical child. You are now in the process of changing an old pattern of beliefs around money. What did you discover on Day 7 about your money pattern? It is crucial that you understand this pattern and unravel it because it is the foundation of the matrix you have built and continue to live within. As discussed previously, your money pattern covers more than just money. It holds foundational beliefs about your ability to get what you want at any level, about your ability to *earn*. Take a look at the definition of the word "*earn*":

1. *To gain especially for the performance of service, labor, or work;*
2. *To acquire or deserve as a result of effort or action;*

Money, of course is the most obvious level of earning, but you also strive to earn respect, to earn success, to earn friendship, even to earn love. Everything you reach for and work to obtain, is affected by your foundational earning pattern. If you aren't yet clear on your earning pattern go back to days Six and Seven and work with it some more. Changing beliefs around earning is critically important to bringing about change in your finances, but also change in so many areas of your life. One way to understand the pattern is to look at your life and see how successful you are at getting what you want:

1. Do you find that you work hard to get what you want, but nothing happens?

2. Do you work hard, slowly building success, and just as you start to make progress, everything seems to slide backwards unravelling all the success you created?

3. You work and work, create the success you want and something comes out of nowhere to take it all away.

These are just some sample patterns that can also be painful realities. They can, however, begin to shift as you start taking them apart. Yet, even if you are successful in dismantling the pattern, there is still one thing that can continue to sabotage all your successful work and that is: *fear*.

Fear has been defined as many things, but we know it is an emotion that may or may not be based on fact. If someone breaks into your house, it will frighten you, but you can just as easily be frightened just thinking about the possibility that someone will break in. It's the emotion that freezes you in your tracks and if you've suffered painful experiences (which of course, we all have), you have memories of pain, hurt, and loss that are now intertwined with your beliefs about earning.

Fear is a powerful emotion. Following the pleasure-pain principle, which one do you think will win? The idea of all the fun you can have with great riches is stimulating and exciting, but is it enough to overcome a belief rooted in the fear that reaching your goal will create loss or pain or humiliation? More than likely there are memories around reaching your goal that are frightening you based on prior experiences where you stretched and reached beyond the norm, only to crash and burn! These memories are not insignificant. Perhaps you have memories as a little child reaching for a cookie and getting slapped. Such memories may certainly cause you to be hesitant in reaching for what you desire, but if you reached for a cookie and the whole house blew up in flames, you will probably never reach for a cookie again!

There have been lots of events that have happened where you

DAY 26

reached for what you wanted and failed. Your earning pattern is the foundation of your money issues and is based on early conclusions you made about your inability to get what you sought from your parents. On top of that, however, there are additional experiences where you sought something and failed and the failure was incredibly painful. If you are like many, you piled judgments on top of the failures and then punished yourself. Now, years later, the memories you have around reaching for what you want, particularly reaching far beyond what you normally allow, is filled with fear. It's time to explore the fear and move beyond it!

First, it's important to identify the fears that may be interfering with your ability to achieve your goal. An easy way to do that is to close your eyes and imagine you have already manifested what you desire. Imagine it is here, happening right now. Make it as real as possible and notice how you feel? Of course, there are feelings of excitement, but is there also anxiety? Are you feeling uncomfortable? Are you feeling frightened?

Now, expand the result of having what you want. If what you are seeking is great wealth, imagine you have triple of what you ever imagined you could have. Imagine you have billions of dollars – not just millions. How will this money affect your life? Do you fear that there will be any side effects? Do you fear that achieving this goal will affect your relationships? Career? Spirituality? What fears come up? Do you fear that people will treat you differently? Do you fear people will pretend to be your friend just because you are wealthy? Do you fear that family and friends will hit you up for money? Do you fear that you will be different, perhaps less kind or less loving? Will this change ripple outward and create other changes in your life?

Sometimes, the impact of achieving what you want is frightening because you've long identified yourself as who you are without it. Does this change scare you because you won't know who you are anymore? It may even relate back to very old messages you received from significant people in your past that succeeding means you hurt someone else or make others angry. Perhaps you know your closest friend resents people with money, so you fear if you are wealthy, you'll lose an important person in your life. These are important fears to acknowledge and release.

As you review the possibilities, tune in to the feelings that come up. More than likely, you will notice there is something big down at the bottom underlying all the excitement and potential, that is holding you back. If you haven't been doing the exercises or putting a lot of energy into this work, perhaps this is the reason. You fear it might work!

What holds you back from creating everything you want isn't the thing you are seeking, but is, rather, the fear of what may or may not happen as a result of your success. In truth, you aren't really afraid of having a million dollars. You are afraid of the repercussions or consequences that having a million dollars may represent. If, for example, you fear your friends will respond negatively to you if you become wealthy, it's not your friends that are holding you back. What is holding you back is the fear of your friends' reaction. Ironically, your friends probably don't even know about your intention to manifest a million dollars, but, the fear will block your intention just the same.

To be successful at manifesting change, no matter what that goal may be, you need to be internally congruent with your goal. Saying you want something isn't enough! You must line up all your inner parts so they are all in agreement with your goal! One little fear is all it takes to keep your positive intentions from manifesting. Fear keeps you from becoming a vibrational match for your desires. No matter how scary it may seem, you need to look it straight in the eye and find out what it wants and why!

Have you ever manifested something with ease? If you even have to think about an answer to that question, that shows how effortless it was.

DAY 26

You already know when you want something, it manifests easily if you are 100% in favor of it. To manifest what you desire, it is imperative to eliminate the fears that conflict with your intentions. If there is no fear in the way, your intentions will manifest easily. But, if there are any fears in the way, there is nothing that is going to allow those goals to come into manifestation and remain in your life. Either you will never manifest it at all or, you will manifest only to watch it all be taken away! To eliminate fears, there are four steps:

1. Discover what fears are there and express them
2. Understand the "why" behind the fear
3. Eliminate the beliefs that hold the fear in place
4. Process and release the fear out of existence

Fear can often feel almost insurmountable to overcome, but that's only because fear *scares* you! In fact, any one of the above steps can eliminate a fear. Sometimes just facing it and seeing what's there is enough. If not, then understanding where it came from and why it shows up can be enough. If not, then do Step Three and ultimately Step Four. If you have a big fear that always seem to come up around money or around any goal you are attempting to achieve, more than likely, it frightens you so much that you haven't even done step one. If the fear is huge, you need to do all four steps.

The steps below are designed to help you move through the most challenging of fears. Don't let your *fear* of facing your fear stop you because once the fear is moved out of the way, you WILL get what you want! It's certainly worth it!

1. Get clear on your fear. This first step is the basis of any effort to process fear or, likewise, any constricting emotion that may hinder you from achieving any goal, and that is, you need to know exactly what you are facing. You need to get clear on what it is. An easy way to do this is to write out your fears. You can write in your journal or you can open your laptop or I-Pad and just type, eyes open or closed. It's not what you say that is as important as just saying it. Start out by simply saying something like this:

> *I have to write out my fear even though I don't know what it is. I just know that it scares me. I want to manifest money, but when I think about it I can feel the tension in my body. Why does it scare me? I don't know, but maybe it's because as a kid I wasn't allowed to have what I wanted. Maybe it's because ....*

Don't worry about what you write or how you write it, just let it flow. Let the words come out no matter how silly or nonsensical they may seem. You can read it later, but for purposes of the exercise, just let the fear speak and express itself in any way it comes out.

2. Find the "why." Once you have given yourself permission to express the fear and all the thoughts and feelings behind it, you are ready for this next step, which is to figure out the "why" behind the fear. Though the fear itself may not be logical, there will be a good and logical reason that created the fear in the first place. If you were scared at the age of 3, for example, at the sound of a noisy airplane toilet, you may never be able to use an airplane toilet for the rest of your life. As an adult, you think this is ridiculous, but that judgment doesn't change the fear that stops you from using an airplane bathroom. Once you uncover the reason "why," you have empowered yourself with knowledge and now can make a different choice or, at the very least, go about the work you need to do to eliminate that fear from your life. Once you have identified the fear and expressed it as shown above, take the time to think about the "why". When you have discovered the "why," you can forgive yourself for the fear and then change it. Write what you discover in your notebook or journal.

DAY 26

3. Eliminate the beliefs. If you have completed both Steps One and Two and are still feeling fear, then this next step is important because it means there are beliefs (probably more than one) that are holding the fear in place. Using the same example above that airplane toilets are terrifying, you may also discover a belief that "being afraid is weak" or even a belief that "fears are difficult to eliminate." Such beliefs are going to undermine the work you've already done. On Day 8, you were given a powerful technique for instantly changing beliefs, called "Changing Room" technique so use it to assist you here. You may have your own process for eliminating unwanted beliefs so use what works for you. Find what beliefs may be in the way of releasing the fear and release each of the beliefs too.

4. Processing through the fear. This last step is not a last resort, but one that will work best if you've already done the first three steps. Processing means meditatively finding the root of the fear and changing it in the *inner worlds*. This is powerful for any fear of any kind. Once again, using the example above of being afraid of airplane toilets, you can re-experience the initial event in meditation and change it there. In meditation, go to the event when you were a child and perhaps flying for the first time in an airplane. How old are you? Two, maybe three years of age? Get inside the mind and body of that little child and feel how the fear comes up. Observe how those around you handle the situation. Do they ignore your fear? Do they make fun of you then and for years thereafter? Follow the exercises in the next section to move through and process fear.

EXERCISE 26

MOVING THROUGH AND BEYOND FEAR

1. Get clear on your fear by writing non-stop whatever thoughts you have about your fear. Just write and write and write in your journal or notebook or type and type and type. Don't worry about spelling or grammar or even what you are saying. You are giving your fear an avenue of expression. So just let it express itself. You can read and analyze it later.

2. Figure out the "why" behind the fear. Once you have identified the fear and expressed it as shown above, take the time to think about the "why". Why are you afraid in this situation and perhaps not in another? What conclusions did you make about life, about your world or about yourself that hold the fear in place? When you have discovered the "why," you can forgive yourself for the fear and then change it. Write what you discover in your journal.

3. Release limiting beliefs by finding what beliefs may be in the way of releasing the fear. Use either the Changing Technique or whatever other belief changing technique works for you. Write what you discover in your journal.

4. Processing means meditatively finding the root of the fear and changing it in the inner worlds. In meditation, do the following steps:

   a. Imagine you go back in time to the initial event that caused the fear
   b. Re-experience the event exactly as it happened
   c. Feel all the feelings and thoughts that occurred at the time
   d. Help this younger "you" release whatever feelings and

EXERCISE 26

thoughts they have by having them talk back, scream, cry, punch, and yell.

5. After they release the emotions, change the incident by giving them the response they want. Perhaps they just wanted to be held and hugged and told it was okay. Perhaps they wanted to be taken off the airplane. Even if it seems unreasonable, give them that outcome. It is your meditation. You can do anything you want!

6. Come back to the present and test the result, imagining a present day event where that feeling may come up and seeing if you feel and respond differently than you did before.

7. Evaluate and understand what you experienced; the significance of the event; the beliefs you formed and of the changes you have made. Forgive yourself by understanding "why" you have been reacting the way you have. Write what you discover in your journal.

DAY 27

HOLDING THE FREQUENCY

If you worked with the exercises yesterday, you should be on your way to manifesting more and more of what you want. Fear in any form will freeze everything, especially if you are afraid to have what you want. But now, you can get back on track to building your resonance again. Remember in that first week how exciting it was? You wrote a Statement of Desire which is your long-term goal. That Statement should be read every day, twice a day, even after the course is long over. This type of repetition is something you've been doing all your life, only, more than likely, you've been saying the things you don't want. When you investigated your money mentor, you probably discovered they are consistently positive. It makes sense that they would have to be positive to generate the incredibly over-the-top-success they have created and continue to create!

If you start paying attention to it, you will realize that you are always talking to yourself and often it is negative self-talk. It's time to take charge of that so you can accomplish your new long-term goals for great wealth. It is also important to repeat positive affirmations all the time so you can allow and create the immediate shifts you want to experience now. If you

DAY 27

are always worried about money, those thoughts are probably something you repeat over and over again. To override such constrictions and fears, it's important to keep repeating the new goals; to keep your focus steady on what it is you want. Remember, super successful people never let go of their goals. That is how they got where they are today! Tom Cruise would still be a struggling actor with a mediocre side job if he had set anything less than super stardom as his goal. The secret to mega-success isn't just desire, or talent, or luck, it is sticking to a goal without ever letting it go. Note the quote from Winston Churchill at the end of chapter 18 where he says: *"Never, never, never give in!"*

Remember, you must have a *burning desire* to have great wealth or whatever your ultimate goal may be. Combine that with the magical tools you have been learning and you can and will succeed! It takes discipline to override the old patterns and put new ones in place, not just for 30 days, but for the rest of your life.

Of course, along the way you will hit resistances. Things come up in the living of life that can veer you off course. It's not possible to maintain a high resonance consistently every minute of every day, but the more you can make it your natural state, the better your life will be. Even Bill Gates has bad days, but that doesn't mean he loses his status as a multi-billionaire. It's not about being perfect, but creating a status quo of abundance that you maintain as a constant part of your normal day-to-day living. You know how to process and program, but if you truly have a burning desire to obtain your goal, you will get back on track as soon as possible. Conscious manifesting comes about as the result of maintaining a resonance at the same level of what you want to create and keeping that resonance going for the rest of your life. I guess you have to say, you just might have to continually be happy! Not a bad way to live!

So, let's get excited again about your goal. You set a long-term goal that maintains the big picture, but you should have also set a more realistic goal for the short term. The long-term goal is what drives you. It is the catalyst that keeps you motivated. Imagining living in your beautiful ocean front estate, or driving your dream car, or traveling the world sharing your talents and skills is what reminds you to stick through the little bumps on the road. And, the shorter-term goal is what excites you each day, especially as evidence of success starts to show itself.

In the first week, you were encouraged to focus on the big picture. What is it you want? What does it look like to be ultra-wealthy? Perhaps you've been visualizing a beautiful, multi-million-dollar house because this image stimulates excitement and anticipation. Don't forget these goals. Even though fear may come up, process through the fear and get back to your dream –visualizing it, feeling it. Even if limiting beliefs show up in your reality as obstacles or blocks to accomplishing your goals, don't let them stop you. You have some powerful tools to change beliefs. If challenges are showing up in your reality, it is because you ARE getting closer to your goal and whatever is in the way, must be removed! Winners never quit, remember?

So, here we are on Day 27. You should have quite a bit of intimate knowledge about your money pattern, about limiting beliefs, and about your self-image around money. You should be working to continually stretch your money image, continually expanding it, feeling grateful, and manifesting evidence of changes in your life. If not, find the fear or any other beliefs that are stopping you. Achieving your goal of great wealth is totally in your hands! It is only a belief away!

As you are resonating on the excitement of being a multi-millionaire, also resonate on the closer, smaller goal which may be, for example, "$100,000 by December 1st." If you maintain this resonance, it WILL manifest because that's the Law! Your physical reality is a manifesting machine because every single thought and every single feeling will

DAY 27

manifest, if you keep it going long enough. Look at your life! It is constantly showing you what you are thinking and feeling!

With the excitement going again and with your goals in mind, there are several other things you can continue to do daily to keep on track and to train your mind and your subconscious to stay focused on the new future you will achieve. There are two things that can augment your drive to achieve and that is:

(1) to develop and expand your relationship with your Future Self, and

(2.) to develop a mantra that you can repeat no matter what might be happening in your external reality.

These two things are powerful tools to add to your daily work. At the beginning of this book, we recommended that you connect with a positive future where, at the end of your life, you are appreciating and evaluating all the success you have achieved in your life. A TV character on a recent television show responded with this statement when his partner looked at him and said, sarcastically: "In your dreams."

"Look at my life! All of my dreams come true!"

Can you make that your response too? Your Future Self can! Though your rich, abundant future may not seem real enough to you right now, your Future Self can be one of your most powerful tools. They have already achieved the success you set in motion only 27 days ago. They may have screwed up, lost focus and fallen down, but they also picked themselves up and kept motivated. You do realize there isn't any great secret key to creating success, right? It simply requires sticking to the program! Those that hang in there and keep going, no matter how many times they may fall down, are the winners. Tom Cruise never gave up. He never quit. Same is true of your money mentor and any other mega-successful person out there. Check it out and you will see that the one thing they all have in common is they never quit! For some, it may take years. Jim Carrey visualized a $10 million check and it took 10 years to manifest! But do you think he cares now how long it took? He spent 10 years building a focus and consistency that is now a major part of who he is! You can do it too! Your Future Self has already traveled this road and can be your greatest cheerleader. They know what it is to get discouraged, but they also know the rewards are worth it. Get to know this Future You. Add them to your daily repertoire of Unseen Friends who can guide you when you hit a cross-road or when a difficult decision needs to be made. Because they've already experienced it, the choices are clear and easy for them. They can be an elegant guide for you and your assured success!

Secondly, add in a daily affirmation or mantra that you can repeat throughout your day. The great thing about a mantra is you can repeat it no matter what might be going wrong in your day. You can repeat it when you are scared, angry, happy, or sad. Although emotion is a powerful additive, your subconscious is always listening to you and to what you say inside your head. Even if you feel like the world is caving in, you can still repeat: "I am loved. I am a super success. I always get what I want." Let's say, for example, the check you needed to bail you out of debt doesn't come as planned. You are panicked and your mind starts racing about all the repercussions if that check does not arrive today. Instead of telling yourself all the things that don't work and *how you never…* – stop yourself and begin repeating your mantra: "I am loved. I am a super success. I always get what I want!" Repeat it again and again and again, even if your heart is pumping; even if your whole reality is trying to show you that you're wrong, repeat it anyhow. Say it just before you fall asleep at night. Say it when you wake up in the morning and repeat it throughout your day. Put it on post-its and stick it all over the

DAY 27

house or office so you are constantly reminded. Make it such a normal, everyday part of your thinking that it becomes habit. Then, watch your reality change. Again, it's not about how quickly the external world changes, but the consistency with which you are building your new reality, your new future. Like any workout routine, you need to be consistent to build new "muscles" and to strengthen the old, weak ones. Dedication + Consistency = Results!

Athletes are often our best examples of dedication and hard work because their goal is very clear and specific as are the steps to get there. You may not be working to build big body muscles or to run a marathon, but your goal is no less significant or less attainable. In fact, your goal may be more difficult to accomplish because you don't have masses of people in agreement with you to achieve this goal. In many instances, you may have people in your life who intentionally knock you down, who are jealous of your achievements, or who make fun of your metaphysics. Even so, there are things you can do daily, a daily mental workout, that can keep you focused and on your path to reach your goal. Once you get moving in a positive direction, there is a momentum that can assist you. If you continually look for evidence of your success, no matter how small, you will see that you are moving forward.

The biggest factor in any success, no matter what the goal, is your mind. In fact, the only thing that is blocking you from amazing, outstanding success is your mindset. That is why it is so critical to pay close attention to what you are thinking, what you are saying, and what you are doing daily. It is important to remind yourself daily to read your Statement of Desire, to do your visualizations, affirmations, and meditations, and to take what action is necessary to get closer to your goal. Confer with your Higher Self and Guides. Get guidance and ideas from your Future Self. Repeat your mantra.

Create a workout routine that works for you. Perhaps every night

MONEY MAGICALLY

before you go to bed, visualize yourself driving your dream car or living in your dream house. You can listen to a recording or you can visualize anything you want on your own. You are already doing it all of the time! Now, you are just doing it consciously.

Though the television character described above may be fictional, there is no reason you can't make his statement one that is real for you:

Look at my Life. All my dreams come true!

EXERCISE 27
HOLDING AND BUILDING A MONEY FREQUENCY

1. Dialogue with your Future Self. In this exercise, you will be communicating directly with the Future YOU who has already achieved great wealth. You can do this as a meditative exercise or simply write a letter to your Future Self. In this letter, ask them to describe their current life to you. Where are they living? What kind of life are they leading and what did they do to get there? If you are currently in debt, ask your Future Self to tell you what they did to get out of debt. If you are unsure of your avenue for creating wealth, ask them what they are doing and how they made that decision. You will be amazed at the amazing answers you can get to any question!

2. Create a Mantra. Create a mantra or affirmation that is a summary of what you want to create such as: "I am rich!" "I am healthy, wealthy and wise." "Every day I am getting richer" "Every day I am getting closer to my goal of great wealth." "Every day I am receiving more money than the day before." Make it something positive that has a bit of discomfort to it, but not too much. It should stretch your belief system just a bit, but not too much that you resist.

3. Set up a Money Workout. Write the specifics of what you plan to do each day to reach your money goal (how much and when.) include such things as reading your goal statement out loud twice a day; visualizing at least 2 times a day, writing a letter to your subconscious once a week and meditating on your goal just before you fall asleep. Set up a specific mental workout routine that you stick to every day until money starts showing up in your reality.

DAY 28

DEVELOPING AN ABUNDANCE ROUTINE

Today is four weeks since you started this program. Congratulations because you are well on your way to changing how you relate to money. By sticking to this program, you have demonstrated some powerful qualities that can carry you through to achieving any goal, the most important of which is sticking to the course!

Yesterday, you were guided to develop a mental workout plan, putting together specifics of what works for you. In two more days, this program will come to an end, but that doesn't mean that you stop working to build your resonance and a continually growing mindset of wealth. You can set up your own reminders and ultimately create a routine. A routine is a series of events that you repeat again and again. If you truly want to create wealth in your life, you need to create a daily routine that shifts your consciousness to a resonance of wealth. You've been working with that for the last four weeks and should already be establishing a routine of what works for you.

Scientists say that it can take 30 days or more for a new habit to be formed. If you have been consistent with this program, you have been working daily to understand and shift your money pattern, to change limiting beliefs around money, and to consistently lift your resonance to

DAY 28

one of wealth. But just because this 30-day program is about to come to an end, that doesn't mean you should stop your new habits or go back to the way things used to be. To assure your new habits continue, it's important to set up a routine of what you will follow from here. At the same time, it's probably a good idea to remind yourself of your old patterns, so that if you find yourself slipping, you can stop it immediately.

There are several things that you learned and that you have been working to change so that your money resonance can rise higher and higher. The following is a list of things you have done these last 28 days:

1. made a commitment
2. built a money resonance
3. discovered limiting beliefs
4. created a "burning desire"
5. visualized your ideal day
6. discovered your money pattern
7. altered your pattern around earning
8. released limiting beliefs
9. built a money resonance
10. reprogramed your subconscious
11. moved past resistances
12. made it real
13. expanded your self-image
14. integrated conflicting parts
15. learned manifesting secrets
16. know you deserve
17. focused on a positive future
18. stayed motivated
19. created avenue for manifesting
20. let your Higher Self guide you

21. remembered to be grateful
22. kept going
23. created your new character
24. found a money mentor
25. wrote a new script
26. moved past fear
27. held the frequency
28. developed a routine

The subconscious mind is one of the most powerful tools you have. It is like a garden. If you continually fertilize, water, and plant the right seeds, it will produce a great harvest. Consistently plant positive abundant thoughts in your innermost mind to build and maintain your wealth resonance. Your thoughts create your world. Your ability to manifest wealth and success each day depends on the extent to which you can think and feel abundantly.

EXERCISE 28

CHANGING YOUR PATTERN

1. For today's exercise, create a chart listing all the things you notice about your old money matrix on one side and listing all the things about your new matrix on the right side. Make note of the differences so that you can continually focus on building and expanding the new matrix.

Old Money Pattern	New Money Pattern

2. Once you complete the chart listed in step 1, create a routine that you will follow daily for at least 10 days. Then create a new routine with additions and changes that you will follow for the next 10 days until each part becomes so automatic that you barely think about it. Eventually you

will notice you are manifesting a different level of wealth than when you started. In your journal, make a list of at least 4 new things you will do every day in your new money routine.

DAY 29

SELF-FORGIVENESS

You have passed the three-week mark and, if you have been consistent with the exercises in this book, you should be seeing some progress in your money reality! If not, then there is one last thing that is worth checking out. Is there anything in your past (or present) that you may still be holding onto that you need to forgive? Don't let your logic get in the way here. Often, the things that we can't forgive don't make any sense to our logical mind such as a marriage falling apart, even though your spouse cheated on you or getting cancer or losing someone you love to illness. It is not uncommon to blame yourself for painful events that happen in your life, just because you feel so powerless and blaming yourself seems to give a sense of control. When a spouse or partner cheats on you, you want to find answers and sometimes the fact that the other person was just a jerk, isn't enough. If there is a lot of pain involved, then the self-blame can be even bigger.

Society tells us to forgive the other person, but rarely are we told to forgive ourselves. What should you forgive yourself for? How about for allowing that deceitful person in your life in the first place. Or perhaps for not seeing evidence that this person was unfaithful or untrustworthy. Sometimes there are judgments that you make because of your lack of

DAY 29

progress, for example, being angry at yourself for procrastinating or taking so long to get over a painful event or even anger at yourself for not succeeding with this course. These conclusions have nothing to do with logic. They have to do with upbringing, beliefs, and personality traits. These judgments are killers when it comes to self-love and allowing yourself to revel in the bounty that great abundance can allow.

Finding the answer to these questions, usually involves some deep inner work, but is well worth it in the end. Why is forgiveness so important? Believe it or not, regardless of how big your money struggles may have been in your life, there is a subconscious knowing that money will bring rewards and eventual happiness. If you believe you are a bad person, or are undeserving because you've made stupid or unforgiveable mistakes, then you certainly are not going to allow yourself to receive rewards and happiness. In such a situation, there is only one way out: *Forgiveness,* not just of others who may have hurt or betrayed you, but of yourself.

As with many things, forgiveness starts with acknowledging what you need to forgive. Are you holding onto any pain from your past? Are you holding onto anger or hurt because of something someone did to you or, of something you may have done to someone else? Is there an event or incident in your past that haunts you and never quite goes away? Now is a good time to start writing out the memories that may still be carrying emotions that have not been released and to get to the bottom of whatever may be holding you back from truly forgiving yourself and allowing love, and money, to flow into your life.

Forgiveness does not mean that you must reconcile with anyone who may have hurt you. Forgiveness in this instance is solely for you. Its purpose is for you to find peace by recognizing what happened, by acknowledging what your role may have been in the incident, and coming to peace with it. The event is over, often long over, so what is left are unresolved feelings that can stay with you forever, unless you deal with them. If you are still holding on to hurt or pain from past incidents, self-forgiveness can be exactly what you need to not only release old feelings, but to open the door to allow abundance and prosperity to flow into your life. Past incidents, particularly those upon which you still hold judgments, are like mud inside a water hose. There is no way the water can flow freely if the hose is still plugged up. By forgiving yourself, and those who may have hurt or betrayed you, you are opening the pipeline to allow abundance to flow continuously into your life. Here's a list of steps to follow to find where you may lack forgiveness and can use the process here to ultimately forgive.

1. Make a list of times in the past when you know you were hurt or damaged because of the actions of anyone, including yourself. Include on this list any events, regardless of size. Write down one or two words that reference the event.

2. Review the list with the intent of putting each in order of priority based on the one with the largest charge down to the one with the least. By the word "charge," I mean the emotional feeling that comes up just by a review of the word references you listed above.

3. After you have prioritized each event, take either one of the top two you have listed and write out everything that comes to mind about that incident. Just take a blank piece of paper and start writing. Don't worry about how it reads or what order the sentences flow. In fact, if you type well, you can even close your eyes and just type, letting the words flow however they come out. Once complete, set this aside for the next 24 hours.

4. Open the document that you wrote yesterday and read it for the first time. Notice what feelings come up as you read it. Write down a

DAY 29

list of words to describe the feelings you discover, *e.g.* fear, hurt, anxiety, guilt, shame, etc. As you did above, select the word or words that have the largest "charge" and begin to work with each, one at a time.

5. Process each emotion that you have discovered by doing whatever you need to release each emotion. If it is anger, who are you angry at? Imagine the person or persons standing in front on you and tell them how angry you are. Do the same for fear, hurt, sorrow, and shame. You can do this by closing your eyes and speaking out loud as though they are standing there listening. You can write them a letter. You can pick up a pillow, pretending they are the pillow and hit, kick, and scream at them. Your goal is to get the emotion out so that you can move to the forgiveness stage. But, **this is very important**! Do not try to forgive before you have released whatever emotion is there. Why? Because it just will not work! Any charge that you are feeling is because the emotions are still alive, like an electric current. The way to get rid of the electric current is to release the emotions with the intention of doing so. After the emotions are released, then you can forgive yourself. If you don't follow this process and the emotions aren't released, you risk self-punishment instead of self-forgiveness.

6. Once you feel you have moved through the emotion, realize that your primary distress is coming from the feelings and thoughts that are with you now, not what offended you or hurt you months or years ago. Next, imagine that you are talking to the "you" who is still holding the hurt (or fear, or anger, etc.) Ask them to express to you how they are feeling. Let them talk, vent, and cry. Allow whatever emotion remains to come up and out.

7. Next, ask this *you* what it needs to come to peace with the event or events that need to be forgiven. Listen to what it has to say and then

give it what it wants. No matter how illogical it may be, you can give this *you* what it wants by using your imagination. If it wants the betraying spouse to break down and cry and ask to be forgiven, then imagine that. If this *you* wants to relive the entire incident with an entirely different outcome, then you can give them that too. Remember that with the power of your imagination, you can give them anything.

Keep working with this *you* until you reach a place of change; until you can forgive the entire incident, including your role in it. When complete, write out your experience in your notebook or journal.

EXERCISE 29

THE POWER OF FORGIVENESS

Make a list of times in the past when you know you were hurt or damaged as a result of the actions of anyone, including yourself. Include on this list any events regardless of size. Write down one or two words that reference each event:

Review the list with the intent of putting each in order of priority based on the one with the largest charge to the one with the least. By the word "charge," I mean the emotional feeling that comes up just by a review of the word references you listed above. Rewrite the list in the order of the biggest charge first and the lowest charge last.

After you have prioritized each instance, take either one of the top two you have listed and write out everything that comes to mind about that incident. Just take a blank piece of paper or use your journal and write and write and write. Don't worry about how it reads or what order the sentences flow. In fact, if you type well, you can even close your eyes and just type, letting the words flow however they come out. Once complete, set it aside for the next 24 hours.

Open the document that you wrote yesterday and read it for the first time. Notice what feelings come up as you read it. Write down a list of words to describe the feelings you discover, *e.g.* fear, hurt, anxiety, guilt, shame, etc. As you did above, select the word or words that have the largest "charge" and begin to work with each, one at a time.

Process each emotion that you have listed in step four by doing whatever you need to release each emotion. If it is anger, who are you angry at? Imagine the person or persons are standing in front on you and tell them how angry you are. Do the same for fear, hurt, sorrow, shame. You can do this by closing your eyes and speaking out loud as though they are standing there, listening. You can write them a letter. You can pick up a pillow, pretending they are the pillow and hit, kick, scream. Your goal is to get the emotion out so that you can move to the forgiveness stage. **This is very important!** Do not try to forgive before you have released what-ever emotion is there. Why? Because it just will not work! Any charge that you are feeling is because the emotions are still alive – like an electric current. The way to get rid of the electric current is to release the emotions with the intention of doing so. Write in your journal what you experience.

Once you feel you have moved through the emotion, realize that your primary distress is coming from the feelings and thoughts that are with you now, not what offended you or hurt you months or years ago. Now imagine that you are talking to the *"you"* who is still holding the hurt (or fear, or anger, etc.) Ask them to express to you how they are feeling. Let them talk, vent, cry. Allow whatever emotion remains to come up and out. Write out what you learn or discover.

Ask this "part" what it needs to come to peace with the event or events that need to be forgiven. Listen to what it has to say and then give it what it wants. No matter how illogical it may be, you can give this *part* what it wants. If it wants the betraying spouse to break down and cry and ask to be forgiven, then do that. If this *part* wants to relive the entire incident with an entirely different outcome, then you can give them that too. Remember that with the power of imagination, you can give them anything. Keep working with this *part* until you reach a place of change; until you can forgive the entire incident, including your role in it. Write out your experiences in your notebook.

DAY 30

OPEN YOUR HEART

As this program comes to a close, there is both a sense of sadness because it is ending, and also a sense of celebration at having successfully completed it. This training, unlike many classes you may have taken in school, isn't so much about learning new information as it is about applying what you already know by practicing, practicing, practicing. Today, as we near the end of this 30-day program, we add one additional component. If there was only one thing to learn and do in all your life, it is this:

Open your heart to love and be loved.

This book has focused on manifesting greater wealth in your life, but the truth is, you are always manifesting. Every thought, every feeling and every belief creates an energy flow that attracts its likeness. By focusing on money and your desire to resonate on more and more of it, you naturally lift your energy field. In time, you begin to exude an energy of confidence and attract more and more positive experiences into your life. Love is the highest frequency there is. Any time you have attracted success and happiness into your life, it has been because you opened to receive. You were, no doubt, feeling loved. You were being loving. And, if for some reason, you were unable to remain in that loving, giving place, it was only because of interfering beliefs. You could beat yourself up for that but, you know that never works. Criticism, judgments, and anger will never provide the freedom and happiness you seek. You know this and so you continue to clear out the blocks. Sometimes it seems like the same ones over and over, but the goal is always the same: *allow yourself to be loved!*

On day 21, you added the component of gratitude to your manifesting repertoire and when you did, you should have noticed a shift in your energy immediately. That is because gratitude shifts your perspective so you begin to look for the places where love appears in your life. It lifts your spirit and augments your energy focus of manifesting what you want. Opening your heart may be the missing piece that pulls this whole program together. If you haven't yet manifested what you specifically desire, it is only because something is getting in the way of letting yourself be loved.

In truth, that is what all this work is about. Manifesting great wealth allows you to receive the bounty of life. Wealth in truth is not a thing, but an energy. It is a state of consciousness that opens you to receive! The more you open, the more you receive! It is as simple as that!

In this book, you are being guided to put your focus on what is outside, but to do this you already know you have to alter your money consciousness from the inside. If you've ever read the book, *A Course in Miracles,* you'll be reminded that it is your internal experience that is important and that you are continually in a place of choice: to choose to experience love or to experience fear. When you make a commitment to create an internal experience of love, you will attract more love. Though it is almost knee jerk to look at our external experiences to feel better, the adept manifester knows it is the other way around. You need to first feel better in order to manifest external experiences that reflect it.

Today, sit back and reflect on all you have learned over the last 30 days. Daily exercises, daily visualizations, and daily meditations are only reminders to keep you on track, but the dedication, the intention, and focus came from you. You did it and can continue to do it. Love and appreciate yourself for what you've done. Love and appreciate your success. Love yourself for the qualities you have demonstrated and are demonstrating that make you a winner: commitment, focus, dedication, discipline, motivation, gratitude, and now heart!

It is not true that there is anyone in the world who is unlovable or unworthy or undeserving. These are beliefs that were formed from false conclusions a very long time ago and which you are now ready to heal. The sole reason you want to heal these things is so you can open to receive ALL that life has to offer; so you can ultimately receive ALL THAT IS.

Start today by shutting down the negative voices and turning to receive the love that is available at every turn. In truth, you deserve to Have It All and to do that you need to open your eyes and see that it's been sitting there all along. Like hidden jelly bean eggs on Easter Sunday, they are everywhere if you just look!

To open to receive more money in your life, open your heart by acknowledging there is a higher power inside you right now. Open to this ever-present Source of love that is everywhere around you. Each day, open to your personal connection with this omniscient presence within you. Spend just a few minutes each day sensing this presence and then throughout your day, ask this inner connection to bring your desired goal into form. Allow love to flow into all situations and events in your life. Sense love flowing to the grocery clerk, the angry gas station attendant, and the new package you just purchased on Amazon. As this inner knowing of love and connection with the All That Is expands and progresses, you will begin to experience amazing results. Develop a relationship with love because it is everywhere around you. It exists in all the things in life. Receive it. It's sitting there for the taking!

Dream Journal.

You may already have a habit of journaling. Perhaps you have a diary or place where you write out your thoughts, all beneficial things to do, but a dream journal expands your journaling to something more. A Dream Journal holds all your dreams and more.

It is a place where you write out your dreams, of course, but also where you put photos, magazine clippings, and newspaper articles of things in alignment with your dreams. It is a place where you open to the Muse within to fantasize about what's possible. You can buy a beautiful bound writing journal if you like or you can use a three-ring binder and add your own pages. The goal is to have a place to jot down your dreams, your yearnings, and give open expression to your heart's desires. Write or copy poems. Write out lyrics to your favorite songs. Stir the Muse within - that part of you that knows how to dream and express the dreaming through words or pictures or art or music. You can still have another book for journaling the day's events or for writing out angry thoughts. This journal is only for dreams.

This is the place where you can open that part of you that you may have put to sleep long ago. When you do, you may find an inner power that you didn't know you had. Inspire yourself. Love yourself by dreaming and allowing the dreams to become real in your life.

EXERCISE 30

OPENING YOUR HEART

1. **Create a Dream Journal.** Buy either a bound journal or notebook or add pages to a 3-ring binder that you will use to contain photos of things you desire to have, places you want to go, people you want to meet. Write out dreams and yearnings. Add in quotes that inspire you. Add information about people that inspire you. Add poetry and song lyrics that touch your heart. Give yourself permission to dream, express, vision, and fantasize without restriction. In this journal you are going to add all things that stimulate your heart and open you more and more to love. This is a special, private place where you give yourself full permission to dream, express, vision, and fantasize without restriction. Let this heartfelt, Soul-full part of you open and feel free to express!

2. **Open to love.** Love and gratitude overflow and blend together, but they are still different energies. Let love express itself through you as much as possible each day. In this exercise, give yourself just 60 seconds to feel, send, and receive love. Close your eyes and set your intention to feel love in your heart and then allow it to expand through each chakra. Each day, try to extend it for a few more seconds until you are up to 2 minutes, then 5 and then 15 or more. The more you do this, the more you will manifest. Use your journal to write out your experiences.

3. **Sending love.** In this exercise, you will sense love between you and 3 people: (1) a friend you care about (2) someone you know but just feel so-so about and (3) someone you hate or really dislike. To do this, just close your eyes and first imagine the person you care about. Imagine you see this person in your mind's eye and that you are flowing loving, warm, caring energy to this person. Do this for a few minutes, then move to the

EXERCISE 30

second person - the one you feel so-so about. Do the same with this person and with the one you dislike. When complete with all three, imagine that you see yourself and send the same loving, warm, caring energy to yourself. Write your experiences in your journal.

CONCLUSION
MONEY IS MAGIC

Thirty-one days ago you began an exploration of your money values, thoughts, and beliefs. You've learned a lot and are on your way to a whole new level of money in your life. The processes and techniques you have learned and are using work, not only for money, but for anything you want in your life. But of all the things to manifest, money is one of the most illusory! Most often, it is merely numbers on a paper. That paper can be a check, a bank statement, even an invoice and you can make those numbers grow and change with the power of your mind! What's more magical than that!

As you know, you have a money consciousness based on beliefs you formed when you were a very young child. As you also know, beliefs can be changed! So, your beliefs around money can be changed as can the numbers on your bank statement! You can literally alter the numbers on your bank statement, delete and eliminate bills, and continually expand your personal wealth simply by changing the beliefs you hold about what you deserve and what you can have. In order to reach your goal that you wrote on Day One in your Statement of Desire, you must continue to alter and expand your beliefs, stretch your image, and

CONCLUSION

program your subconscious with acceptance of yourself as a wealthy person. All of this is done with one intention in mind: to clear your thoughts and feelings so you can focus with consistency on what you desire. You shouldn't expect to accomplish all of this in only 30 days, but 30 days of refocusing and deliberate intention, can make a dent in your old programming. Your subconscious is starting to understand that you "really do want to change this" and your Money Consciousness is now changing!

Any fears you may have around expanding your money relationship are based on old messages and old conclusions. Keep exploring! Keep expanding! Keep stretching! This book is a little step in a big direction. From here on in, you can continually step up to learn more and be more when it comes to money and the avenues you create to generate money. Money is a mindset. Where were you 30 days ago, and where will you be in six months or six years?

You can transform your life by keeping your focus on lasting wealth. When your goals begin to manifest, use your excitement to build momentum, to keep creating and continually expanding. Ideas and dreams you wrote about in the first few days of this course, can become more real. As your wealth expands, you will develop and create more avenues for greater money flow. You will begin to work with and inspire others with your personal life changes. You will learn to work smarter and develop a strong mindset of abundance for all, knowing there is plenty for everyone. You really can create your own charity, buy an island, or even build your own hospital. There are people already doing all these things. They are no different than you. They just think differently!

Turn your life into a money machine! A Magic Money Machine. Create a method for generating your money consciousness and holding your focus. If you want to create $1,000, focus on it. Feel it and create it. Then do it again with a larger sum. The richer you think and feel, the more you will attract. And when you're operating from that place of gratitude, it creates a different experience. The more successful, wealthy, and grateful you become, the more momentum you can gain. Other people become attracted to you and add to that wealth with more deals, more opportunities, and more experiences that lead down the path to great riches. Wealth truly does start in the mind and heart. Once you've locked that truth into your psychology, the financial freedom that was only a dream can now become your reality!

Make sure you use this 30 days of practicing as a new foundation to keep going forward. Eternal vigilance is the price of success. You can completely change who you are in relationship to money and you can do it MAGICALLY! These four steps are essential to manifest money magically:

1. Know you are powerful
2. Be courageous and daring enough to use your power
3. Focus to create a money resonance
4. Trust in your ability to create ALL you desire

With this as a basis, you can construct an ideal lifestyle, an ideal home, ideal friends, and an ideal environment in which you live. You are not restricted in any way. All it takes is willingness and a desire to keep pursuing your goals. Thought is the most powerful thing in the universe. It has the power to magnetically draw on the infinite bank of prosperity! Keep your goal sharp, definite, and unwavering, focusing on what you want until you KNOW it is yours.

You are on your way to a whole new future and you will manifest what you envision. All you must do is remember that if you are creating it the way it is now, you can create it the way you want it to be. Keep your focus on what you want and where you are going!

CONCLUSION

A Magician's Life

There are multiple components to becoming a successful manifester and you have all the keys in your hands. True magic is the ability to "use extraordinary power or influence to produce exactly what you want - when you want it." You have been manifesting things all your life, but being a true magician means you can do this consciously. Can you imagine desiring a check to come in the mail for $4000 and having it arrive the next day? Can you imagine setting a goal for new clients and having it come to fruition within seven days? Can you imagine receiving a million dollars in income and manifesting it within a year? Within six months? Within a week? If you answer "no" to any of these questions, then go back to the beginning and start this course over again. Each of the things listed above are possible and available for you to achieve. It starts with imagining! It's maintained by expanding the imagining! And, it ends by imagining! Imagining what you want, then expanding the imagining to enhance and lift your resonance and then imagining that it is a done deal! The more you do this, the more successful you will be. And, the more you practice, the more adept you will be at creating all you want! The ultimate is to consciously create what you want ALL the time and when you can do that you are living a Magician's Life!

Congratulations for sticking with the program. It will be very exciting to see your successes expand and your life change as you become more and more magical in all you do! Thank you for participating. You officially graduate today!

Happy Millions!

APPENDIX I
Visualization

Visualization is a powerful process of "seeing" in your mind's eye what it is that you want to create. Jim Carrey visualized a check for $10,000,000 and ultimately created exactly that. Olympic athletes see themselves doing a particular sport over and over again perfectly until their body automatically does it exactly that way. Pro-golfers practice the perfect stroke until their brain (and subconscious) know exactly how to do it no matter how much pressure they are under. You can do it too. As Jim Carrey said to Oprah, *"Visualization works, but you have to work at it. You can't just do it once and think you will be successful."* Your mind does not know the difference between what is "real" and what you create in your mind, therefore, the more "real" you make your visualizations, the more successful you will be. This means to bring in every sense - see the money, feel it in your fingers, smell it, flip it through your fingers so you can hear it. This is the same way that your mind measures reality and you can use it to create anything that you want. But, the ultimate key to success with any visualization is repetition. Do it regularly and often - just like the pro-athletes do and you will succeed!

Below are a series of suggested visualizations that will become more successful as you repeat them as often as possible. Pick one or two that work for you. Repeat it and watch for the magic that can result!

1. *"Expanding Wallet*

Start by imagining what your wallet looks like. You can even take your wallet out and examine it with detail. Notice the style, the texture, the color, the stitching. Where is it worn or frayed? Open it and see the inside where you place the paper money. Examine the paper bills and their details as well, the color, feel, smell, etc. Now, close your eyes and imagine you can see this same wallet and the bills inside. Imagine that

APPENDIX I

the wallet is packed full of paper bills and that the wallet keeps expanding as you are adding more and more bills. Imagine that the denominations of the bills keep increasing. $20 bills (or E20), then $50 (E50), $100 (E100), $500, E500. $1000, (E1000). How does it feel to know that your wallet it holding thousands and thousands of dollars (or Euros)?

Make sure you enhance the feeling! This is very important. The whole purpose of visualizing all of this money is for the feelings that is generates. Those feelings are the resonance that will change you and your reality.

2: "Stacks of Money"

In this visualization, you imagine that you are stacking gold bars all across the floor. To help you visualize and imagine, take a look at photos of gold bars on the internet. A gold bar weighs approximately 27 lbs. (12.4 kg) so they are very heavy (about the same as 4 gallons of water.) You have to lift and place each bar with effort. They are heavy and extremely valuable. Each one is worth around $380.

On top of the layers of gold bars, you then place stacks of paper bills. The cash is wrapped in individual stacks of about 1" - 1 1/2" thick. Each stack is wrapped with string or with a paper band. You neatly stack the paper bills on top of the gold bars, layer after layer. Money is piled high all across the room.

Imagine that you are layering these bills everywhere in your room. Put the bills inside of cabinets and drawers; on top of closet shelves. Fill the bathtub to the top with cash; the shower; the closets. Keep expanding this visualizing to all areas of your house - the garage - even your car. Imagine that when you drive, paper bills are flying out of the windows (but you don't care, because you have so much of it.) Imagine that you have paper bills in your pockets, your brief case, your purse. Money, money EVERYWHERE!

APPENDIX I

Use photos to help you imagine these images. Do this visualization each morning when you wake up and again before you fall to sleep at night.

APPENDIX II

Affirmations

We tend to make affirmations unconsciously, and since our words become reality, our affirmations have the power to create great changes in our life. Here's some suggestions for positive affirming statements you should get in the habit of repeating to yourself regularly.

- I am grateful for the wealth I receive and am receiving
- I am a multi-millionaire worth $_____
- Everything I want comes to me in abundance
- I am overflowing with wealth and riches
- Money comes to me easily and effortlessly
- Everything I do is successful
- I am grateful for the continuous abundance in my life
- I have a golden touch. Everything I touch turns to gold
- Every day I become more and more wealthy
- Wealth is pouring into my life daily
- My great wealth gives me peace, happiness, and joy
- I am blessed with all the abundance and wealth in   abundance
- I am always seeing opportunities to make more money
- Money comes to me from multiple resources all of the time
- I always have more than enough of everything
- I am incredibly rich!

APPENDIX III
How Rich People Think

Take a look at the difference in beliefs between how rich people think and how poor people think. According to author Steve Siebold, these differences are critical as far as creating and allowing wealth. Which ones apply to you?

HOW POOR PEOPLE THINK:	HOW RICH PEOPLE THINK:
focus on saving	focus on earning
think about money in linear terms	think about money in non-linear terms
hard work creates wealth	leverage creates wealth
money is the root of all evil	poverty is the root of all evil
being rich is a privilege	being rich is a right
money is complicated	money is simple
rich people are crooks	rich rich people are ambitious
building wealth is solitary	building wealth is a team effort
worry about money	dream about money
believe money is negative	believe money is positive
rich people are shallow	rich people are strategic
money changes people.	money reveals people
the road to riches is paved with formal education	the road to riches is paved with specific knowledge
money is earned through hard labor	money is earned through thought
worry about running out of money	think about how to make more money.
think about spending	think about investing
see money through the eyes of emotion	see money through the eyes of logic
underestimate the power of referral marketing	know referral marketing creates millionaires
focus on activities that give them pleasure	focus on activities that make them money

APPENDIX III

HOW POOR PEOPLE THINK:	HOW RICH PEOPLE THINK:
see money as a finite resource	see money as an infinite resource
earn money doing things they don't like	get rich doing things they love to do
rich people are ruthless	rich people are generous.
have a lottery mentality	have an action mentality
wait for rescue from financial mediocrity	know that no one is coming to the rescue
believe rich people are smarter	believe rich people are savvy
see money as controlling	see money as liberating.
work for money	work for fulfillment
believe you have to do something to get rich	believe you have to be something to get rich
play it safe with money	take calculated risks with money
you have to have money to make money	believe in using other people's money
believe in financial scarcity	believe in financial abundance
see money as a weapon	see money as a tool
having a job is the safest way to earn	outstanding performance is the safest way to earn
see money as a weapon	see money as a tool
believe they aren't worthy of great wealth	believe they deserve to have great wealth
deny the importance of money	money is a component of life
money is their enemy	money is their friend
wait for their ship to come in	build their own ship
financial markets are driven by emotion and greed	financial markets are driven by logic and strategy
money is about status.	money is about freedom
live beyond their means	live below their means
equate money with stress	money gives peace of mind
think small	think big
believe people are out to get them	believe the world is out to help them

APPENDIX III

HOW POOR PEOPLE THINK:	HOW RICH PEOPLE THINK:
thinking is unrelated to their net worth	thinking is the catalyst of all results
experience good fortune and can't believe it	experience good fortune & wonder what took so long
the more money you earn, the more stress you have	the more money you earn, the less stress you have
the more money you make, the more problems you have	the more money you have, the fewer problems you have
the rich are obsessed with money	the rich are obsessed with success
rich are selfish & self-absorbed	the rich are self-absorbed
dream of having enough money to retire	dream of having enough money to impact the world
believe it's shrewd to be cynical	believe it's shrewd to be optimistic
rich people are snobs	rich people guard themselves
believe rich should support the poor	believe people should be self-reliant
see the wealthy as oppressors.	see the wealthy as liberators
rich is outside their control	getting rich is an inside job
the rich think they are more intelligent	intelligence has little to do with richness
associate with anyone	carefully monitor associations
believe in the importance of advanced degrees	embrace any form of education that makes more wealth
have loosely defined goals with flexible deadlines	have highly defined goals with do or die deadlines
work as little as possible.	work as smart as possible
love to be comfortable	are okay being uncomfortable
are timid and scared	are aggressive and bold
long for the good old days	dream of the future
set financial expectations low so won't be disappointed	set financial expectations high so are always excited

HOW POOR PEOPLE THINK:	HOW RICH PEOPLE THINK:
play not to lose	swing for the fences
have a financial windfall and worry about losing it	have a windfall and figure out how to leverage it
are externally motivated to make money	are internally motivated to make money
have a consciousness of lack	have abundance consciousness
believe people seek money for power	believe people seek money for control
see no connection between money & health	believe that money can save your life
ambition is a sin	ambition is a virtue
rich people are arrogant	rich people are confident
self-made millionaires have an unfair advantage	self-made millionaires know their advantage is hard work
base their beliefs about being rich on the minority	base their beliefs about being rich on the majority
believe they're missing something.	know beliefs make the difference.
believe they lack desire	know everyone has all they need
must choose between family & wealth	know that everyone can have it all
believe having a job gives security	know there's no such thing as security.
starting a business is risky	a business is the road to wealth
a small group shouldn't hold all the money	the wealthy welcome the masses to join them
wealth creates dysfunctional families	poverty creates dysfunctional families.
money creates corruption	lack of money creates corruption
rich are spiritually bankrupt	the rich are very spiritual people
if you become wealthy, you'll lose friends	being wealthy expands your network
you must sacrifice health to get	being rich will make you

APPENDIX III

HOW POOR PEOPLE THINK:	HOW RICH PEOPLE THINK:
pass their limited beliefs about money to their kids	pass their unlimited beliefs about money to their kids
teach their children how to survive	teach their children how to get rich
teach their kids about money by example	teach their kids about money by example.
encourage their kids to be nice and make friends.	encourage their kids to be smart and build a network.
teach their kids to be happy with what they have	teach their kids to go for their dreams
teach their kids that money isn't important	teach their kids the importance of money
teach their children the games of the masses	teach their children the games of the wealthy
don't believe in personal development or self-help.	believe self-help is the secret to getting rich
don't see a connection between travel and wealth	travel connects them with the wealthy
have access to social skills of the masses	have access to social skills of the refined
would rather be entertained than educated	would rather be educated than entertained
rich people are workaholics.	millionaires have a ton of fun
focus on money only when they need it	focus on money all of the time

All rich people – poor people quotes are from Steven Siebold's book, "How Rich People Think", London Press. 2014

Anne Sayers is a Transformation Coach who is dedicated to assisting people to reach their Truest Self. She lives in Thousand Oaks California and can be reached through her website: www.annesayers.com. If you'd like to purchase meditations and visualizations that go along with the chapters in this book, go to www.annesayers.com/shop